MONOTHEISM

Oxford Centre for Postgraduate Hebrew Studies

MONOTHEISM

A Philosophic Inquiry into the Foundations of Theology and Ethics

Lenn Evan Goodman

THE AMERICAN PHILOSOPHICAL ASSOCIATION

DAVID BAUMGARDT MEMORIAL LECTURES

ALLANHELD, OSMUN • PUBLISHERS

ALLANHELD, OSMUN & CO. PUBLISHERS, INC.

Published in the United States of America in 1981
by Allanheld, Osmun & Co. Publishers, Inc.
(A Division of Littlefield, Adams & Company)
81 Adams Drive, Totowa, New Jersey 07512

Library of Congress Cataloging in Publication Data

Goodman, Lenn Evan, 1944–
    Monotheism, a philosophic inquiry into the foundations
of theology and ethics.

    (David Baumgardt Memorial Lectures; 1978)
    At head of title: Oxford Centre for Postgraduate
Hebrew Studies.
    Includes bibliographical references.
    1. Monotheism—Addresses, essays, lectures. I. Oxford
Centre for Postgraduate Hebrew Studies. II. Title.
III. Series.
BL221.D38   1978   210s [212'.4]   79-24818
ISBN 0-86598-068-3   AACR1

81 82 83 84 / 10 9 8 7 6 5 4 3 2 1

Printed in the United States of America

CONTENTS

OXFORD CENTRE FOR POSTGRADUATE HEBREW STUDIES

THE OXFORD CENTRE FOR POSTGRADUATE HEBREW STUDIES is designed to foster Hebrew and Jewish studies from the biblical period to the present time. Among its aims is the encouragement of individual and collective research projects.

The Centre is under the academic aegis of Oxford University, but is financially independent and administered by its own Board of Governors.

The Centre awards Visiting Scholarships to distinguished scholars and junior fellows to enable them to pursue their studies in Oxford and to conduct courses and seminars on Hebrew and Jewish topics.

The books in this series were written following a period spent on the Yarnton Manor Estate, and are published under the joint auspices of the Oxford Centre for Postgraduate Hebrew Studies and Allanheld, Osmun & Co.

PUBLICATIONS COMMITTEE

N.S. Doniach   R.A. May   F.G.B. Millar   D. Patterson   G. Vermes

Foreword and Acknowledgments

The American Philosophical Association
David Baumgardt Memorial Lectures, 1978

David Baumgardt (1890–1963) was educated at the Universities of Freiburg, Heidelberg, Vienna and Berlin, where he took his doctorate and was subsequently Professor of Philosophy. He left Germany without permission in 1935 to go to Spain, where he participated in the celebration of the 800th anniversary of the birth of Maimonides. From Spain he went to England, where he was Visiting Professor and Research Fellow at the University of Birmingham. Coming to the United States in 1941, he was briefly on the faculty of Pendle Hill near Philadelphia, and then served as Consultant in Philosophy to the Library of Congress until 1954. In 1955–56 he was Visiting Professor of Philosophy at Columbia University, and during that year gave the Matchette Lectures at Columbia on "Great Types of Western Mysticism: Their Lasting Significance."

Baumgardt's published work was extensive. His doctoral thesis was on Kant, and his early work mainly on Spinoza. He took an interest from the beginning in Jewish philosophy as such, with essays on Moses Mendelssohn, for example, as well as on Maimonides. But his professional field was ethics, and during his residence in England he came to take a profound interest in the work of Jeremy Bentham, which led to one of his principal books, *Bentham and the Ethics of Today,* Princeton, 1952.

Toward the end of his life, Baumgardt made plans for a fellowship at the Hebrew University of Jerusalem for the purpose of encouraging "an impartial, well-reasoned discussion concerning the justification of the Judaic morality of love and justice in opposition to the morality of sheer power and to the Christian ethics of all-forgiveness . . . avoiding any unjustified superiority complexes and unwarranted opposition . . . No adherence to my ethics required, but emphasis should be placed on a critical examination of a topic as yet much neglected, for which a basis has been laid in my work." Although such a fellowship was in fact established, Baumgardt's widow, Mrs. Rose Baumgardt, felt that there was a need to establish a new lectureship more fully to facilitate philosophical inquiry into the areas of Baumgardt's chief philosophical concerns and interests. Concise formulation of the focus of those interests was given by Philip Merlan in a footnote to one of the last articles Baumgardt submitted for publication before his death: "Baumgardt attempted to reconcile the ethics of force with the ethics of love, describing his own philosophical position as that of a Benthamian hedonist . . . systematic ethical and religious problems underlay all of Baumgardt's historic research." (*Journal of the History of Philosophy,* December, 1963). The new lectureship established to further philosophical inquiry into these areas of concern was entrusted to the auspices of the American Philosophical Association.

The author wishes to express his gratitude to Mrs. Rose Baumgardt for establishing the David Baumgardt Lectureship, to the American Philosophical Association and their selection committee for electing him as one of the two first recipients of the Baumgardt Award, to Dr. David Patterson, President of the Oxford Centre for Postgraduate Hebrew Studies for his warmth, encouragement and gracious hospitality in providing the auspices and facilities of the Centre at Oxford and in Yarnton Manor, to the numerous students and members of diverse faculties at Oxford for their collegial welcome and for the stimulating discussions he enjoyed with them during the tenure of the lectureship, to R. J. Kearney of the University of Tasmania, Hobart, Australia, to Bernard Jackson of Merseyside, England and to Elliot Dorff of the University of Judaism, who shared their thoughts with those of the author regarding the subject matter of these lectures, to Rabbi David Lieber and the faculty of the University of Judaism, including many former teachers, for welcoming him there for a trial run of some selections from these lectures, and to Miss Renee Kojima and Mrs. Floris Sakamoto for their care in typing the lecture script and the present revised version. The last thanks go to the author's wife, Dr. Madeleine Goodman for her never failing encouragement and practical inspiration in the possibility of the good life.

As a result of a national competition among American philosophers, Lenn Evan Goodman, Associate Professor of Philosophy at the University of Hawaii, was selected to share the Baumgardt Award with the California ethical philosopher Herbert Morris. Goodman's studies of monotheistic philosophy date from his student days at Harvard, where he received his B.A. summa cum laude in Philosophy and Near Eastern Languages and Literatures. He pursued these interests at Oxford, where he was a Marshall Scholar and received his D.Phil. in 1968, and over the following years in his researches into ethics, metaphysics and religious philosophy. His Baumgardt Lectures on Monotheism and Ethics were delivered at the Oxford Centre for Postgraduate Hebrew Studies in Oxford and at Yarnton Manor January 17, 18 and 19, 1978.

THE LOGIC OF MONOTHEISM

The concept of God is that of a being of absolute or infinite perfection. The truth of this contention can be established by linguistic and conceptual analysis, although not perhaps by linguistic/conceptual analysis of the usual sort but rather by analysis of a dynamic or dialectical sort. For in common usage the term God, like most philosophically interesting words is used in a variety of senses, some contradictory to others and some incoherent in themselves. Through a Socratic process which batters these usages one against another, some coherent notion of divinity can arise. From this it is discovered that by the divine is meant something which is special, extraordinary, something with which strong feelings and powerful energies are associated, or rather, to put the matter more closely in terms of the subjective intensions of the users of this sort of language, something in which powerful values—for energies here are values—are vested. Gods are the superhuman creators of nature or of culture, the manifest or unsuspected causes, sources, grounds, essences or identities of natural processes and properties, of human motives and characteristics and of the human motives and characteristics which are projected upon the world and to whose efficacy the salient or arresting features of the natural and social cosmos are ascribed.

The pan-animist, who experiences nature in accordance with the notion articulated by Thales, that all things are filled with gods, is affirming not the ordinariness of the divine but the extraordinariness of all things in nature. Epicurus, who denied the providential control or influence—interference he would have said—of the divine in nature or in human affairs, moral or social, argued for the non-concern of the gods on the grounds that what is blessed and immortal need not or would not trouble itself or trouble others.[1] The linchpin of his argument is the assumption, shared with his presumptive dialectical adversary, that the divine is to be thought of as immortal and as blessed beyond the human state—that is to say as transcending some of the imperfections of the human condition. The conclusion, that the gods are indifferent and unconcerned with nature or with man, is simply the working out of some implications of that transcendence. Similarly, when Plato argues in the *Republic* that the gods are not venal beings to be won over with words or propitiated with offerings, and when he takes issue with the poetic and mythic representations of divine beings as human-like personalities possessed of human strengths and weaknesses of character and displaces the mythic gods philosophically with his own divine beings, the Forms, it is to the perfection of the divine that he makes his dialectical appeal. It is impious to represent the gods as less than perfect beings, unworthy of their divinity, to express the same point in terms with which common religiosity can readily find common ground.[2] For even the most anthropomorphic of myths assigns to the gods exalted natures, a stature and appearance beyond the human norm, a special aura of divinity or nimbus by which divine presence (if unconcealed) is unmistakable. And those fables (as opposed to myths) which treat of gods in purely human terms plainly do not speak religiously of the divine*—or rather they do not speak of the divine at all as such, for to speak religiously is to speak of the divine as divine, which is to say, as our examples show (along with many others), to speak of something extraordinary either in experience or beyond it.

For the tribesman who intuits a special presence in the well or spring, an awesome terror in the fever which afflicts his wife or son or a power in the stirring of lust or fear or laughter in himself, it is plain that the divine is something extraordinary.[3] So too in the sense of the vastness of the sky or of the ocean. Experiences of this kind have been labelled[4] *"mysterium tremendum,"* a term which has some descriptive value *vis à vis* the experience, provided it is not entirely overlooked that such experiences differ in kind; and some no doubt, are *sui generis*. Here too, then, at what might be regarded as the very origins of the concept of the divine, divinity is that which is experienced or regarded as extraordinary, regardless of where that extraordinariness is experienced or how it is differentiated from other possible experiences of related kinds. The concept of divinity from its inception is a value concept.

---

* Fables of this sort thus have an extremely crucial cultural function to perform, for they are in effect the first and often the only accessible or acceptable expression of the overtly secular tendencies—that is of the inclination to treat all things as ordinary and reject, or set aside the extraordinariness of the divine.

The intuitive sort of experience, in which the most primitive logically of all forms of awareness of divinity is found, is not at all incompatible with the absence (or non-application) of many of the central logical and metaphysical categories upon which conceptual thinking depends. Notoriously, the distinction of self from other, of subject from object, of class (tribe, species, kind) from particular, of cause from effect, of a thing from its name or a whole from its part or of any such category from any other is at best extremely fluid in the most primitive types of mythic expression of the experience of the divine.[5] For this reason it is not surprising that the line of demarcation between the notion of the divine and its surroundings in experience is initially unclear. The logic of myths, like that of dreams is associative. The nexus between one event or experience, character or trait and the next is not syntactical or causal in any way that reflects the order of conceptual thinking of (disinterestedly described) natural events. Rather it is an associative nexus, in which the imagination, ungoverned by conceptual restrictions (or at least ungoverned for the most part by any uncompromisable conceptual commitments) springs from one arresting feature of experience to the next with no more motive cause for stirring given or expected than that which it discovers or invents in the kindred features of the objects it confronts. Small wonder that from the perspective of such a mode of experience all things seem to be filled with gods. For surely to the lively sensibility there is no feature of experience which does not in some regard, at some time, in some circumstance, from some point of view, take on the excitement of the extraordinary—Thus the (secular) aesthetics of Zen and the celebrated remarks of eastern sages to the effect that the highest phase of divinity is contained in the lowest specimens of natural things—the Godhead itself in the shrubbery at the bottom of the garden. What such remarks express is the ubiquity—not necessarily omnipresence, but the ubiquitous potential for encounter with the divine, *i.e.* the extraordinary, even in the most ordinary things.* Nor

---

* Zen resists the hypostatization of a transcendent source for these experiences, seeking to focus rather on the experience itself and to retain the locality of the extraordinariness of the experience in the object, or (with more metaphysical subtlety) in the experience itself. Zen is in this sense at once the most pagan, the most secular and the most purely aesthetic (non-referential) of religions—qualities which contribute to the interest it arouses in the West today. Yet it is a religion, nonetheless, in virtue of the sense of the extraordinary which it locates in experience, and which it expresses symbolically in numerous ways through its own aesthetic of action and encounter with events. Only if it became wholly indifferent to experience, not merely detached but bored, would Zen cease to be a religion. It is the absolute pluralism of such an approach, its total refusal to integrate the various aspects of experience in value hierarchies or conceptual systems which renders them conceptually unstable and always liable to displacement from the pragmatic sphere—unless artificially maintained as a kind of ritual/moral pose. There will always be this danger to pure secularity when it strives to constitute itself into a religion—that by placing all values

should such ubiquity seem surprising, for the encounter is as much a product of subjective response as it is of objective effect. It is not merely energy or splendor, etc., which produce the AH! or the AHA! of religious experience (which may be enshrined or indeed transmitted in poetry and art) but energy or splendor (including destructive energy and the awesome splendor of peril and death), etc., *perceived* as such. Which is to say, it is not energy, splendor, etc., in themselves but these aspects of things *perceived as values,* which coalesce into the experiences upon which is founded the notion of the divine.

But the aboriginal value content of the notion of the divine on an experiential level renders the concept itself restless, and it is this internal conceptual dialectic which leads (in time inevitably) to that concept's rectification by a process we can follow conceptually in Plato's arguments that the divine is not venal or Epicurus' that the blessed and immortal is not meddlesome, or anthropologically in the unfolding of religious history in the displacement of baser and more homely gods by ever nobler and more transcendent gods. When Xenophanes holds it anomalous that the Ethiopians' gods should be black and those of the Thracians red haired and blue eyed,[6] the source of the discomfort he intends to create is the discrepancy between human partiality and definitude on the one hand and the perfection which Xenophanes is sure the notion of divinity will evoke in the mind of a religiously inclined audience. From here it is only a step to the denial of definitude *vis à vis* the divine, a step actually taken by Xenophanes' alleged disciple and genuine heir, Parmenides.

The seminal equivocation of Parmenides upon the verb 'to be' by which metaphysics was founded as the science of being as such and reality united in a single, unique, invariant and in principle un-differentiated divine Being, was motivated by an uncompromising unwillingness to allow the partiality of being. Reality either was or it was not. This fundamental either/or was not equivalent with our pallid copy of it in the principle of contradiction which holds only that a given particular state of affairs must either be or not be at a given time in a given sense or respect. For here there were no thoughts of particularities and no concessions that 'being' might be in different senses or respects,

---

on a par it will leave itself no grounds for the wonder and excitement which lie at the core of all religious experience—that by valuing all things equally it will have set all at nought. A parallel danger exists for the monotheistic religions, which are of transcendental type, that by placing too great a gap between the world and God, the world will be emptied of those very properties which prompted the first furtive or longing glances in the direction of the transcendent and become a wasteland of alienation, vanity and anomie. Zen addresses this problem by discipline and aesthetic rhythm and (controlled) variety; monotheism, by the endeavor not to lose hold on its primal insight, that the world is the expression of the creative energy located in the transcendent Divine.

or even at different times. What is just is and cannot not be. It cannot be now and not be later or be in one regard and not in another. Being here is absolute and absolutely rules non-being impossible and unthinkable.

So powerful was the intuition of the absoluteness of being and its uncompromisability by any plurality of subjects, predicates, times, aspects or regards that the followers of Parmenides, the Eleatics and Megarics and even the Stoics, continued to champion the law of contradiction in militant opposition to what they saw as Aristotle's qualification to it, the rule against equivocation, long after the original elenchus had been exposed and the issue in principle had been settled, at least to the satisfaction of their opponents. What was at issue really was the unwillingness of the Parmenidean heirs to part with either the ultimacy and absoluteness of reality (and the corresponding ultimate and absolute unreality of negation) or the equation of ultimate reality with divinity.

Recognizing the phenomenological untenability of absolute monism (since even an illusion of plurality and change involves a real plurality and a real change) and its logical weakness, since it was predicated on the too radical dichotomy between utter reality and utter unreality (and thus built monism on the premise of a tacit dualism), Plato had compromised (in the *Sophist*), allowing a kind of partial negation and partial affirmation, which turns out to provide the language necessary for the delineation of the features of the phenomenal world. And Aristotle had followed, dividing nature analytically, conceptually, into those aspects which could be described unequivocally scientifically, in virtue of the presence of the Forms, and those per accidens relations and the ultimate Platonic "otherness" of matter, the unnamable substrate of the forms, which could never be the subject of scientific inquiry. The divine was elevated (in some "regards" at least—to the chagrin of the Eleatics and the Stoics) out of nature to become ultimately, in the neo-Platonic synthesis, the monadic source of the Forms. In this wise the unity of the Parmenidean One was *in some measure* or in some "respect" preserved—but at the same time compromised. The heirs of Eleaticism could hardly be expected to have been pleased. What they had spoken of was the uncompromisable absoluteness of being, and their motive was an intuition of the absoluteness of the divine.[7]

Because divinity is a value notion, the refinement of moral notions leads inevitably to the refinement of theological notions. Hence the discomfort of Hesiod with the divinities of the heroic age: Hesiod does not share the values celebrated in the Homeric epic.[8] It is the moral ferment which is characteristic of all human life and whose subtle but telling nuances mark the most significant changes of human history that keeps theological concepts changing. For, like Epicurus, who made his gods gentlemen of leisure and paragons of ataraxia, and like Aristotle who made his god a self sufficing and all-energizing intelligence, we fund all that is best in ourselves and our ideals into our concepts of divinity. Such is the logic of that idea.

But the dynamic of values is such that this funding of values from all sources into the concept of divinity does not continue indefinitely, leaving merely a congeries of disparate gods each representing some manner or another of experiencing the extraordinary in all its manifold forms. Rather there is an integration, called for by the values themselves, based on the recognition that perfection itself is imperfect unless it is absolute. It was this call to the integration of values and equation of divinity with the absolute that had motivated the Eleatics. And they had not been the first to feel its evocative power. The gods of the sky and justice triumph inevitably over the tellurian or sylvan gods of terror or panic fear, since justice can rule, preside, create order where divinity per se (in its minimal sense) can only peer forth from its lurking places. The same synthetic trend which transforms the amorphous aura of the extraordinary, the magical energies of mana and the undefined sensations, intuitions and emotions of naive (*i.e.* untutored) experience into coherent (if often somewhat unpredictable) personalities, forms, objects, and events does not content itself with such degrees of integration but plays off against one another the values it has defined in its divinities and so, by modulating them against one another while continuing to project the intensionalities of human experience upon them, molds them into personal gods who symbolize and even articulate both verbally and in their social intercourse with one another the values which they stand for[9]—values whose celebration is no longer left to the private and primitive intuition, but whose celebration now is instituted, *i.e.* routinized in standard, identifiable symbols, canonized in standard, recallable and reliable words, ordered in festivals whose seasonal recurrence ensures rhythmic recapitulation of some surrogate of the divine experience at intervals fixed to mitigate the conflict of one set of celebrated values (and divinities) with another and which seeks to assure that the experience itself will not be lost.[10]

The definition of the values which are centered in the gods is heightened mythopoetically by the use of contrasts. Hence the interplay of those values is dramatic. That is to say their diverse modalities are dramatically projected as conflicts among the gods. For the gods attain definition as persons and heightened definition as persons whose aims conflict, that is not merely as persons in story but as persons in dramatic conflict. And just as the histories of the gods come therefore to represent human moral conflicts, those same conflicts, projected back upon the human condition (magnified by their projection on the gods in myth) become conflicts amongst the heroes in epic. The essential difference between epic and melodrama is that where melodrama pits virtue against vice, epic pits virtue against virtue—the cunning of Odysseus against the power of Ajax or the candid warlikeness of Achilles. The outcome of the contrastive method which literature and art employ to heighten the values they present—which means, of course, to heighten the response those values may produce—is the pitting of every virtue against itself, and all the rest, as in the tragedies of Sophocles, which arise out of the Homeric epic by the pressing to the extreme of the virtues which that epic celebrates. The trial (or agon) of the tragedy is the testing of the limits of each human virtue; and the resolution of that trial is the recognition of that limitation. The meaning of this resolution (or rather failure of resolution!) is that expressed by the conundrums of the sophists: There is no good in absolute terms but only 'good at . . .', 'good for . . .'. What is good in terms of the piety of Antigone is not good in terms of the statecraft of Creon. Even human wisdom, pressed to the extreme, finds its limits, as Oedipus himself, as human wisdom's paragon, comes to illustrate and to know. Wholeness eludes the tragic hero as it had eluded the heroic gods, whose value content the tragic figure lives in drama.

And so the matter might have rested, for some time, so far as Greek thought was concerned, had not Socratic dialectic uncovered the unity (that is the inseparability) of the virtues, sensing that courage could not be stupid or piety dishonest, or love meretricious or unwise. Anaximander had described a conflict among the natural elements or "principles" of things, but behind that conflict he had sensed an equilibrium, which like the Zeus of Cleanthes did not disdain to be called justice. Heraclitus had found a logos behind the inconstancy of change, a principle both willing and unwilling to be called Zeus, just as Pythagoras had found harmony in opposition. But it was Socrates who proposed, partly by what he said and more impressively to Plato by how he lived and died that tragedy was not inevitable but that human goods could coexist, moderated by one another, under the governance of reason, and produce a life unmarred by internal conflict and a death which was not the result of the human breakdown of values too strongly stressed but the natural consummation and fulfillment in its courage and serenity of the internal harmony it expressed.

The recognition of the possibility of resolution to the conflicts which had been heightened for the sake of drama and effect in epic and tragedy was the awakening of Plato and led to his further synthesis of the Socratic unity of the virtues on a metaphysical level with the absolute unity philosophically deduced and framed in poetic modes of expression by Parmenides, the One, Plato's Form of the Good or God, which became for Plato the source or ground of all being, transcending in its absolute perfection all diversity and change.

The discovery, Plato tells us,[11] of this highest Unity is the outcome of dialectic (*i.e.* of the method Socrates had practiced and by his practice taught)—that is to say, the testing of our concepts. But it is not dialectic which gives us the experience of that discovery, for that experience is intuitive, a consummation of the integrative, synthetic work of consciousness and reason rather than a stage in the progression of that work. As an intuition, and an intuition of Totality, that experience is ineffable. But Plato points to it in language borrowed from the mystery cults, whose celebrations sought to capture and assure (in public and reproducible form) the experience of the divine—and very legitimately does Plato borrow these institutions' terms (but not their assumptions or conventions) since the experience he speaks of is that of the Divine as such, *i.e.* the fully integrated concept of the extraordinary—transcending time, diversity, multiplicity, change, partiality, prejudice or inclination—transcending personality and all the energies and values of things, their partial goods and partial unities, their equivocal realities and identities, which in the light of this experience are now regarded as mere expressions of the full reality, absolute perfection, complete unity and truth of the One.

Experientially Plato's beatific or ecstatic experience is of a piece with the primitive modes of awareness which it integrates, the most naive modes of consciousness of the extraordinary. But philosophically it is superior, for now the experience is interpreted and itself provides an explanation for all the rest. As a result, all modes of knowledge and all dimensions of ethical and aesthetic experience acquire places in the expanded world which the new mode of experience and the new, comprehensive mode of interpreting that experience create. The human virtues become partial expressions of that totality of Goodness. Relative goods are real goods to the extent that they partake of (or express) that unique Absolute Good. So the sophistic paradoxes of relativity dissolve once recognition is accorded to the Absolute Standard in terms of which relativity is predicated, just as the moral conundrums of the tragedy dissolve once it is recognized that the diverse varieties of goodness are not in conflict with one another but are manifold expressions of a single, simplex Ideal, towards which it is the human task to proceed, insofar as this is humanly possible.

Monotheism is achieved by the integration of the concept of divinity, a process never fully completed by Greek philosophical thinkers for reasons which can be stated in the language of a number of different categories of explanation whose compactness in reality may belie the diversity of their modes of expression. Conceptually, the relation of the many and the One was never satisfactorily resolved by Greek philosophers who sought to complete the work of Parmenides, not by the

Platonists and Aristotelians, who exerted the most sustained efforts of the philosophical schools in such a direction, nor surely by the Stoics, who vied with the Academy for the title of true heirs of Parmenides.[12] Theologically, a completed monotheism would have been incompatible with the powerful localism of the most ancient type of Greek religious experience and tradition, a difficulty no different from that encountered with paganism elsewhere, except to the extent that the articulators of Greek culture, Homer above all, had succeeded phenomenologically in transforming localism into an immanentism which could recommend itself even to philosophers whose chief value was the universal and could thereby render them suspicious of too transcendental a view of the divine, which might seem to leave the world and men godless or dead to the vitality of pagan religious experience. Politically, moreover, there was the loyalty to the civil religion, which survived Cynic disparagement to become Roman fidelity in the Stoa (and to be treated with respect even in the skeptical philosophy of Cicero) and was intensified among philosophers in late antiquity as the neo-Platonists (and others, syncretically forgetting not only cultic but school differences) became increasingly aware of the enormity of the challenge posed to pagan ways of thought by monotheism in the early Christian centuries. This loyalty to the gods of the polis and later of the Imperium was as much or more a part of paideia as was philosophy. It was very much alive and to be reckoned with in 410 when Augustine undertook to capture it for the City of God, and it flared into baleful intellectual significance for the last time as a living focus of philosophic loyalty in the final abortive defiance of Justinian by the pagan philosophers of the Athenian Acadmey, which ended in the closing of the nine hundred year old school in 529.

Yet despite the conscious constraints by which the greatest leaders of the Greek philosophical traditions avoided monotheism, the process of integration toward it was well begun by them out of the foundations laid in Greek myth and epic (by the differentiation of the characters of the gods and the delineation of their natures and the logic of their actions), in the analytic work of the Sophists and in the synthetic and integrative insights of Socrates and the pre-Socratics.

The crucial step in the integration of the concept of divinity is the purgation from that concept of certain salient aspects of the experience of terror which were constitutive therein from the origins of the concept. This purgation, which we might projectively entitle the purgation of evil from divinity, or the harrowing of the pantheon, proceeds gradually and piecemeal among the Greeks, crucial stages being represented by the banishment of the Titans, etc., the qualified subordination to Zeus of Poseidon and Tartarus, the inferences of Plato and Epicurus as to the impartiality/uninterestedness of the gods, etc. It is same purgation

Aristotle speaks of, borrowing the term from the mysteries, as the function of tragedy in his magnificent reversal of the field in which he normatively transforms tragedy from a celebration reenacting the terror of the divine (*i.e.* the Dionysiac frenzy) to an ethical performance whose objective is to be the (Platonic) conquest of that frenzy (expressed emotively as empathy and fear) by reason. But theologically that purgation is achieved not by the purgation of the baser emotions from the human breast but by their conceptual purgation from the divine. This Aristotle expresses by his identification of God with what is highest, *i.e.* most removed from privation, potentiality and change, most transcendent of particularity, noblest, most self-sufficing and most capable of moving others without itself being compromised by motion—Self-thinking thought or Intelligence.

The logic of God expresses itself most clearly in Greek thought when Plotinus argues against Aristotle that intelligence cannot be what is most divine, since intelligence is a definite thing distinguishable from others, whereas what is most divine is absolute, unqualified, thus undefinable, or to use a word of which Greek thinkers—even Aristotle—stood in awe, unbounded, infinite. If being is defined in Platonic/Aristotelian wise as coextensive with definitude, then the Plotinian God transcends even being. Its unity, since it engulfs all things and is the source of their reality, is therefore absolute, transcending not time, space and matter alone, but all conception. These facts are known (or can be, although they naturally tended to slip through the fingers of some later Platonists, whose search for ever closer intermediaries to the Transcendent led them into ever more baroque ontologies and ever more bizarre demonologies, while their grasp of the central point led them even on occasion to attempt to raise the Deity beyond the absolute!) through the analysis of the concept of self-sufficiency or from that of unity, or that of perfection—in short through the recognition that the logic of the concept of divinity is intolerant of privation.

The same conclusion, the identification of the Absolute as the divine was achieved within the Hebraic tradition not gradually but at one fell swoop—although the elaboration of the implications of that recognition was not completed instantly or even in the centuries that followed but continued and continues even now. The suddenness with which this recognition was accomplished along with the necessarily concomitant purgation of evil from the concept of divinity was a result of the fact that in the Hebrew canon the theological transformation did not await the development of formal dialectic but grew directly out of the moral consciousness and cosmic aesthetic which the prophets articulated and projected and in which the people shared. There was a dialectic, but a valuative rather than a formal or abstract dialectic. That this is so is evident from the language which is used in connection with the awakening by which evil was purged from the divine: In behalf of Sodom and Gomorrah Abraham is pictured as demanding "Will not the Judge of all the earth do justice?"[13] Here already God is universal rather than local, and a demand is made (not a plea for mercy or refuge taking as in Islam) but a demand addressed less to God than to the (moral) logic of the concept of God. Zeus too was a God of justice and a defender of strangers and guests whose modes of expression in the eagle and the thunderbolt were well known to those who stood in awe of him—just as Apollo visited his worshippers not only with sunlight and the harmony of the lyre but with murrain, Artemis with the arrows of the plague, Athena not only with wisdom but with the ashen face of a virgin's hatred and of war, Poseidon with storm, earthquake and tidal wave. The object, when such terrors threatened, was to learn (if learn one could) the pleasure of the god and satisfy it at whatever cost. For one who questioned the legitimacy of that pleasure there could be no safety.[14]

But here God's will is known. The divine "displeasure" is with human lawlessness (ḥamas), injustice, and an appeal can be made to that very principle of justice which provides the content to the notion of God's wrath. The terror of first stating such a demand must have been immense, but the terror is overcome by a moral courage based on a preceding insight, an inference first expressed questioningly as a hypothesis that God is not unjust, that the notions of arbitrary rule and tyranny have no place in the notion of the divine, or ought have none. "Far be it from Thee to do such a thing as this, to slay the righteous with the wicked, and far be it that the righteous should be as the wicked!" The moral categories are clearly present; the lines between them clearly drawn. There are righteous and wicked persons, and the differences between them are manifest to the human observer, objective, such that God himself, whatsoever His character, must be expected to recognize them as the man of conscience does. So too, clearly drawn, are the differences in deserts. The righteous do not merit death insofar as they are righteous. The immemorial notions of divine punishment and wrath are not to be applied to them, not if those notions are to be understood in terms of justice. For man knows what justice is and knows again what justice must be for God, if God is to be a God of universal justice. It cannot be the setting of the deserts of the guilty and the innocent at parity. Moral consciousness here is fully formed and confident enough in its self-awareness to take on a role as a conscience for God as well as man. Values are no longer subjective, so divinities may no longer make them arbitrary.

The experiences in which men first encountered the energies they came to think of as divine were not all of them terribly pleasant or nice.

Central among them, I believe, was the kill or the moment just before the kill, the moment of truth, Hemingway called it, referring to not unrelated phenomena. The portrayal of this moment forms one of the most prominent motifs of the most ancient art, the pre-historic cave paintings of Altamira and Lascaux, and we can still read the excitement and the energies involved at this climactic moment of the hunt in those works, so vivid was the experience—a clear rival to another quasi-ecstatic natural moment represented in the pre-historic portrayals of the naked female form. This moment, the moment of the kill or the moment of truth and the anticipated kill was filled with power, terror, hunger, desire, longing and danger for those who shared it. It was naturally a locus of divinity and a focal point of celebration and devotion as early as such institutions arose. The cult of animal sacrifice grows out of this moment, and the verb for sacrifice in Hebrew is identical with the verb for slaughter. For the slaying of an animal, even of a domestic animal, was fraught with much the same significance as the slaying of a victim in the hunt.[15] By the associative logic of primitive consciousness the two are one event. Thus with the ancient Hebrews as with the ancient Greeks (so we learn from Porphyry in the one case, from Mishnah *Avot* in the other[16]) every meal was construed a ritual event, and the same rites which dedicated a victim to the divine were used in devoting an animal to the knife or to the table. The formal (or ritualized) meal is not the only survival of the social archaeology of the hunt and the kill/moment of truth. The preservation of hunting (and its values) as a sport, the institution, glorification, celebration of bull fighting, were others—along with the cult of sacrifice itself.[17]

The autonomous horror or terror of the kill, when instituted as a sacrificial cult could reach beyond its origins in the hunt—since it was now a divinity whose will (whether functioning quasi-independently merely by the working out of the logic of the original projection or whether fed constantly by new projections of specific or particular social situations) must needs be served. The outcome in the extreme, should these emotions be left free to seek their extreme, almost inevitably is a demand for human sacrifice—where else would the intensity of the experience produced or the significance of the act be as filled with enormity once the primal experience has become attenuated and the endeavor to relive or recapture it has ceased to be the primary intent? It is for this reason, I believe, that evidence of human sacrifice is not lacking in the documents which make reference to the late pre-history of the Greeks and the Semites, and that evidence and more than evidence of ritual cannibalism and human sacrificial cult is not lacking from the data regarding other cultures.

Thus when Abraham in *Genesis* is represented as receiving a demand from his God to sacrifice his long awaited and favored son I do not believe that the request would have been regarded by the first hearers of this account as seeming at all foreign to their ancestor, although of course they would have expected him to regard that demand with terror.[18] The sacrifice of Iphigenia, although filled with terror, is a matter of course. The human sacrifices associated with the Aztec cult and games are likewise. Indeed, as Levi-Strauss helps us to understand, the logic of game as ritual made them necessary. For game as ritual seeks an equilibrium—often between the living and the dead and therefore often attainable in formal terms only through human sacrifice. Here too the fossil remnants of that ritual structure are far from rare or evanescent or arcane in the superbowls and superbouts of our present culture. Levi-Strauss even goes so far as to state that every victory in sport primordially is a kill: "as all the North American mythology confirms, to win a game is symbolically to 'kill' one's oponent. This is depicted as really happening in innumerable myths."[19] And all the evidence of archaeology and anthropology agree that the reality of this consummation was not confined to myths.

What is remarkable in the Abraham story is the reversal of what I take to have been a rather grisly and (to use Lucretius' word) impious norm. For Abraham is told by God that he must sacrifice his son and by the angel that his test has been sufficient, that it is enough that he has not withheld his son; in other words, that God had only been testing him and had never intended that Isaac should die. "I know already that thou fearest God . . ." God, of course, always knew. He was not to learn from the experiment or trial. Rather the purpose of the trial, as Maimonides tells us, was to demonstrate to humanity (or to Abraham!) the ultimate limit of human devotion.

But how did Abraham know that the angel was to be believed? How was Abraham to know that what God had seemed to demand had at no time been intended? He could not rely on "revelation," for revelation had told him two contradictory things, that his sacrifice of his son was demanded and that he had passed the test imposed by that demand *without* the slaying of his son. Which of these two alternatives was to be believed? It is at this point, not when Abraham stretches out his hand to take the knife, that the crisis comes. Is he to believe the angel who tells him that God's intent was just to test and that the test is over, or is he to believe the prior revelation which had explicitly demanded: "Take now thy son, thine only one, whom thou hast cherished, take Isaac and get thee to the land of Moriah, and offer him up as a burnt offering on one of the mountains which I will tell thee of" (*Genesis* 22:2)? Abraham must decide alone, without further outside prompting; and in deciding, emblematically he decides for all his successors.[20] Looking up he sees a ram caught in the thicket, and impulsively he seizes it and offers it as a surrogate for the sacrifice he has determined not to offer. He gambles on his own consciousness of the truth that God is good, that the judge of all the earth shall do justice. Then he waits to know the outcome. Is he to be punished for refusal of the sacrifice demanded, or was he right to obey the second prompting and withhold it? The confirmatory experience is not long in coming. The binding had been sufficient, the slaying was not required. Abraham was not to be punished but rewarded. "Out of the heavens a second time the angel of the Lord cried to Abraham, 'By Myself have I sworn, sayeth the Lord, since thou hast done this thing and not withheld thy son, thine one and only, I shall surely bless thee, shall surely multiply thy seed as the stars of the heavens and as the sand on the shore of the sea, and thy seed shall inherit the gates of their foes. And through thy seed shall all the nations of the earth be blessed, because thou hast hearkened to my voice." (*Genesis* 22:15–18). With boundless relief Abraham returns to his servants and completes his journey. But what was "this thing" that Abraham had done? He had not slain his son or offered him as a burnt offering.

How did Abraham hearken to God's voice if he did not sacrifice his son? Plainly it was the latter voice which had offered the correct interpretation, that the earlier command had expressed a ruse, a test or trial, or demonstration, as Maimonides expresses it, not a demand intended to be fulfilled. What that voice claims is that Abraham has not withheld his son although plainly he has not slain him. It is possible to give one's son to God, then, without killing him—Indeed, only such "not withholding" is acceptable to God. For Abraham's reward is promised, "since thou hast done this thing and not withheld thy son." But how has he not withheld his son if he has not slain him? Given him in other ways perhaps before the demand for sacrifice or even while the two walked together? Primally, saliently, he has spared him and, *by so doing, given him to God.* The reward is not for blind obedience but for (and through) the creative moral synthesis which sees that giving does not require slaying, but indeed excludes it; the angel seems to be saying that the reward is for Abraham's stedfastness to his conception of God as an absolute in whom there is no possibility of evil. The tenor then would be: Since you made no exception of your son, your one and only, to the universality of the moral law in the ghastly but all too commonplace assumption that the greatest enormity is what would be expected by the Absolute Divinity (and be pleasing and gratifying in the eyes of such a God), for that reason, and through your grasp, communicated to your successors, of the incompatibility of divinity with evil, will you and they be blessed and through that insight will they become a blessing to the peoples of the world, witnessing, in the triumph of the moral law as the universally acknowledged principle of right, their own (symbolical) mastery of their enemies.

As with the Greeks there was a trial, but the outcome was not tragedy but the refinement of conviction. When Agamemnon slays his daughter, it is the will of the divine, but so too is Agamemnon's compensatory betrayal and murder, and Orestes' vengeance, and the vengeance taken by the Furies against him, until at length, as irrationally as it had begun, the train of retributions and violations is itself violated by reconciliation. Here, by contrast, arbitrary violence and terror are debarred from the conception of the will of God. To put the matter from the divine perspective (as the Bible itself does in adopting as objective fact the second revelation and accepting it as the correct interpretation of the intention in the first, when it opens the story of the *Akedah* with the words "God tested Abraham"—*Genesis* 22:1), God had renounced violence and evil. The trial was a testing of conviction not in the sense of a probing of the static intent of an immoveable faith in an unknown but implacable absolute, but rather in the sense of a refining and strengthening of Abraham's nascent conviction.

Conviction here is not blind allegiance to an unknown datum but conscious and increasingly self-confident adherence to, faithfulness in the inner logic of the ideal Abraham had already grasped, the ideal of God as Perfection, which was given practical confirmation by the successful passage of the test and strengthened morally by the experience, as a principle of character—although its logic did not require strengthening. All along what had made possible the emergence from this trial without tragedy was the advance in moral awareness by which Abraham had progressed first to a tentative, hypothetical (but nonetheless, outspoken, even rhetorical) hope edging toward confidence that God, as the just judge of all the earth (morally) must do justice and then to a more confident invocation of the same Lord as the infinite and Universal God (*el 'olam* of *Genesis* 22:33), affording the intellectual basis necessary to the moral test (self-purgation/God-purgation) which was, so far as the concerns of the Torah extend, immediately to follow.

It is the moralization of God, or rather the consummation of the incipient moralization of the notion of the divine by the integration of all values in one being, which renders the God of Abraham universal. For if evil had remained in the divinity—or even the possibility of evil, such that Abraham's question 'Will not the Judge of all the earth do justice?' might have been answerable by any other than the affirmative answer it presupposed—then there would have been the possibility of conflict of principles, one deity or system of deities representing one value or set of values and another deity or system of deities representing another. In such a case no deity could have been absolute or universal. In essence what Abraham came to see, aided by his moral crisis, was that only the perfect can be absolute and only the absolute can be divine. It was this relationship between the absoluteness demanded by the (mature) concept of divinity and the integration of all values, called for by the working out of the dialectic of values with one another, which the *Mutakallimûn* were to voice when they argued that there cannot be more than one God since a duality or plurality of deities would inevitably limit *and therefore conflict with* one another. The language adopted by the Mutakallimûn to express this insight was jejune. But what they were grasping for was valid nonetheless. The possibility of conflict no more comports with the inner logic of the concept of divinity than does the possibility of limitation. But to eliminate the possibility of conflict from the concept of divinity (and thus, ultimately, to eliminate the possibility of limitation) it is necessary that there be an integration of all values, rendering the value system represented by the Deity irrefragable.

It was necessary, in other words, for the proposition 'God is good' to become what we might be inclined to call an analytic proposition—for Abraham's question to lose its meaning as a question in the very course of his asking it, because the only possible answer it could receive was affirmative—for that question to become no longer a question at all but a joke, since the only possible answer was already inferentially expected or known. The proposition in effect is just the opposite of a Sophist's paradox. For there the object is to show the incompatibility of disparate values by pressing those values to a contradiction. But here the joke is in the obviousness of the analytic connection, which expresses itself as a moral incumbency upon God. The judge of *all* the earth (morally) *must* do justice. The very concept of a universal judge requires it. For that concept itself, the concept of universal judgment, is made possible and, in a dialectical sense, necessitated by the concept of universal justice. It is in this way that the integration of all values is presupposed in the formation of the concept of a universal Deity. For only of a universal judge can it be demanded and expected that justice, universally be done. And only through the integration of all values—that is through the seeing through or refutation of the presumption of the inevitability of tragedy—can the possibility of universal justice (that is justice to all) be conceived. If my gain inevitably involves your loss, then we face a no-win game, and the possibility of universal justice, adequate to us all, does not arise. Human sacrifice in formal terms (and the games that share its formal logic, disregarding the material or sensational values either may serve) is in essence the symbolic, public playing of such a no-win game. Similarly, if the adequate expression or fulfillment of one legitimate value inevitably requires the suppression or frustration of another. Thus the logic of tragedy and of Sophists' rationale of exploitation, *i.e.* injustice. But if my fulfillment can be achieved in and through yours and vice versa, through the establishment of community, then there is the possibility of universal justice, and that possibility renders possible (and dialectically inevitable) the demand that the divine as well adhere to its standard. The possibility of such a community is grasped and its realization is legislatively ordained in the global Biblical command that our love for one another be on a par with our love for ourselves—and, of course, by the concrete and specific legislation which gives material content to that law.[21]

But the conception of a universal standard of justice requires the purgation as spurious of numerous false values such as the terror of slaughter and the plague, salacious and meretricious sexual pleasures and the iniquity of cunning, whose precipitation from the concept of the divine is accelerated by the polarization of the universe into opposing spheres—the pure and the impure, the sacred and the profane, the evil and the good—polarities whose conceptual essence is more than tinged with the conceptual colorations of the concept of judgment and justice and the related value notions.[22] Only by this means, whether with Abraham and the Hebrews or with Plato and the Greeks does the concept of divinity become the concept of God. Only through the concept of universal justice, which is integrative of all values which are to achieve acceptance as true values (and purgative of all which are not) does the one God of monotheism become the absolute and sole divinity and do the numerous gods of paganism become nonentities—empty things, to use the Biblical locution, which preserves the identification of the ontic sphere (so far as the divine is concerned) with the sphere of (non-specious) values.

The recognition of the *moral* need for an integration of all (positive) values is not the only means by which the concept of divinity may be integrated. There is, as already mentioned, the inherent logic of that concept as a value notion which militates toward the same synthetic end. And corresponding to the moral thrust toward integration there is a cosmic, cognitive approach as well to the same end—the recognition of pattern and unity in nature, the underlying continuity of causal processes and analogy of causal principles which prompt cosmological speculation. Here at their origins, the foundations of scientific method are at one with those of cosmological monotheism, although the common origin and originally kindred motivation of rationalistic science and monotheistic cosmology have perhaps more often been forgotten than recalled by practitioners of both. The discord of the two with paganism, which both call superstition, is sufficient to call to mind their common origin.

The pagan sensibility, inherently pragmatic, is naturally projective. It peoples nature with social beings, motives and intentions, whether those of spite, favor, malice, concupiscence, greed or love, because these are the counters it believes it can understand and with which it feels capable of arranging some sort of deal or *modus vivendi* which will impart some measure of confidence to an existence predicated upon hope and fear.

From this backdrop cosmological (as opposed to cosmogonic) thought disengages and differentiates itself by virtue of its groping toward objectivity. Its single most distinctive feature is silence (as opposed to projection) in the face of ignorance; and coupled with this negative moment, an intense positive curiosity based not merely on the desire to control but on the desire to know. The constancy of the celestial motions, the recurrence of the seasons, the consistency from species to species and individual to individual of the principles regulating the pattern of life, all belie the notion of the presence behind natural things of capricious, arbitrary or socio-morally contingent occult actors of the sort paganism requires as its interlocutors with the unknown and suggest rather the operation of a coherent scheme or system, operating in accordance with principles of its own, whose pattern is discernible but whose foundation or ground (although plainly monadic, as the evidence of coherency in the pattern suggests) transcends analogy with any human principle, such as that of intellect or design, which may be projected upon it. This monadic ground is the substrate of all philosophic and scientific inquiry; and, conceived of as transcendent and a source or summit of values, of which human moral values and nature's energies and aesthetic values are but the partial expression, it is the goal of monotheistic speculation as well, and the object of monotheistic worship. The peak of monotheistic conception in this regard is the recognition, along with the apprehension of the monadic or coherent character of this Ground or Source, of the inadequacy of all projections of human notions upon it. Hence the silence of *Genesis* not only as to the motives which prompted God to create—envy, ambition, solitude, solicitude for man's sake, etc.—but also as to the mechanism by which creation was achieved—not out of this or that or using this object or that as a tool—and as to the character of God—no talk here of intelligence, benevolent design, desire to test or try men, judge or save (!) them. Creation is purely the stark relationship of the Absolute with the contingent. No further characterization of it is or can be given without resort to poetry. But through the notion of creation, the awesome or reassuring recognition of a sense and hence a unity beneath the surface disparity of phenomena, an integration of values is achieved on the cosmic plane which parallels, reinforces and is reinforced by their integration on the moral plane.

The Biblical conception of God[23] as the Universal Creator is thus not far removed from the conception voiced by Abraham of God as universal judge. I hesitate to assign temporal priority to one of these conceptions over the other, but in fact there is no need. For all created things—all animals and plants, heavenly bodies, all features of nature, "the earth," in fact are values in the perspective we are discussing, that is all are for the polytheist potential loci or foci of divine energy or activity; whereas for the monotheist they are actual loci of the divine expressive (or creative) act. All that is necessary for the sake of integration is a purgation of evil from nature corresponding to the moral purgation of evil from divinity by Abraham. And this is accomplished Biblically again through the idiom of judgment but this time by the projection of God himself (for the sake of objectivity), portrayed in the judgmental role, assaying all the objects of His creation and seeing that they are good. Thus the purgation of terror in nature goes hand in hand with the purgation of terror in the concept of the divine. And God becomes, as it were by the same act of thought, at once the creator and the judge "of all the earth"—and of the heavens as well, since nothing is excluded from the dominion ascribed to the Universal Deity—God is seen not only as the (objective rather than arbitrary) arbiter and standard of all values but indeed their source.

While I hesitate to assign temporal priority to ethical/social over ontic/cosmic integrative moves since from the religious perspective both the ethical/social and the ontic/cosmic realms fall within the sphere of values, it does seem to me that the valuative perspective on action has an immediacy which the valuative perspective on nature lacks. Cornford, I think, may have gone too far, in reading social structures into the early Greek cosmologies[24] pressing the significant parallelism between cosmic and social structures of such schemes of thought almost to the point of a reductionism of cosmic speculation to social imagination. A central significance of the notion of compactness is that these levels, the social and the cosmic, are not seen as distinct but as interpenetrating, mutually interpreting if not fused systems. Thus the division of the cosmos into the "temples" of the pagan heavens or the realms of the pagan earth and underworld is not merely the mirroring of social moieties and the reflection of their symmetries and interdependencies. The social structures themselves, rather, are equally figured on the notions of justice and cooperation among the gods—steps toward a higher integration. And when that integration is achieved in monotheism, the absoluteness of the Deity is not merely the reflection of the idea of universal (as opposed to tribal) justice. The contrary relation holds equally: the ideal of universal justice acquires the sanction of divine authority.

Still there is the primacy of human experience to humanity. Mythical thought and magical practice do project the values of the inanimate world upon the animate and of non-human nature upon humanity, but the more striking projection is plainly that which proceeds in the opposite direction. A king or chief may be likened to the sun, a rock, a tree or beast, but that is only to assign to him, in elevated degree or kind, properties of which he may be naturally possessed. More impressive is the movement in the opposite direction because it assigns to the non-human world predicates which naturalism would reserve exclusively to humans, as when the rock or wood or spring are endowed with life, and affective intentions or animal species are assigned not only temperaments, but personalities and social standing. And it is this striking quality, which goes beyond mere metaphor, which imparts the unique power of myth. Thus it does not seem far fetched to suggest that it is from the social and the ethical sphere, conceptually (rather than temporally) speaking, that the operators are derived which render possible the evaluative treatment of nature and ultimately the integration of the cosmos as a coherent, unified rational system through the integration of the conception of the deity which underlies the disparate energies (read as values) which are evident in nature. Thus it is the social experience of Abraham in the moral realm which mediates the transition for him from his confrontation with (or perhaps accosting of) "the judge of all the earth" to his invocation of "the God of the universe," *el 'olam*—the absolute and infinite, eternal or universal God.

More perspicuously (for "social experience" is far too flat and abstract to signify what must be meant here) it was the confrontation within the family, of the demands which Sarah might make, which Isaac might make, and beyond the family of the demands which all his progeny might make, which provided a motive force for the rectification of Abraham's value concepts and hence the purgation and successful integration of his concept of divinity. Or more broadly speaking, the conception of the God who is Creator of the universe is made possible (and dialectically necessary) by the conception of the God who is the judge of all the earth. Thus in the opening words of *Genesis* God is introduced as the creator of the heavens and the earth. The cosmological extrapolation which assigns to the one God dominion over all that is or might be, not merely over "all the earth," seems to be a direct expression of that sense of universality which results from the conception of God as the absolute and unconfined summation of all (true) values. Thus the spring to the metaphysical, from the known to the perhaps infinitely unknown and unknowable world is made possible by the moral premise which now defines the content of the concept of divinity. If this is what God is, the reasoning seems to be, then no (true) value escapes His dominion, *i.e.* His judgment and indeed origination. It is the conclusion of such reasoning, I suspect, which is expressed in the opening sentence of *Genesis,* and indeed in the entire opening sequences of that book.

Plato followed the same pattern. For it was upon the Socratic unity of virtues that the Platonic unity of Forms was to be founded, the ontic unity not predicated logically upon the moral but recapitulating it and reaching the metaphysical level only with the aid of abstract terminology and argumentative schemata which had been honed in dialectic with the Sophists over morals—their universality or particularity, subjectivity or objectivity. Only on this metaphysical foundation could Plato ground his new cosmology, which fused the elements of the Sophists' false dichotomy of law and nature in the synthetic unity of the seminal concept of natural law. It was only because Socrates (in response to the goading of the Sophists) had brought philosophy down from the heavens and into the streets and market places of the city that Plato became able to restore philosophy to the heavens, and that no longer in the furtive role of an utterer of gnomic conjectures but regnant in conceptual control of that underlying unity the *physikoi* had sought, but which had eluded their insufficiently subtle grasp. Without the mediation of metaphysics or the development of logic as a science in its own right, the Israelites had achieved a comparable and indeed more consistent outcome from the impetus, plainly, of the thrust of moral ideas, seconded powerfully by an overmastering yet wondrously tranquil cosmic aesthetic.

The concept of God, then, that emerges from the Hebraic experience of the divine in the valuative spheres of ethics and the contemplation of nature and which points beyond nature to a wider, cosmic realm of all that is or can be is the concept of an absolute or universal being. It is this concept which Philo fuses with the Greek essays in the direction of monotheism, the conceptual conclusions reached by Plato and the Stoics, for example. And it is this concept the preservation of which Maimonides regards as the *raison d'etre* of the ethnic continuity of Israel.[25] While the exigencies of prophetic mission and the limitations of poetic expression may or must compel the individuals who struggle to voice this concept to "speak of the Creator in terms of His creation," that is to point the direction in which the Reality of God must lie rather than (*per impossibile*) designating or directly signifying that Reality, the logic of the concept is such, Maimonides argues, that the pristine absoluteness of the idea can always be restored by dialectical probing of the (classic Biblical) *topoi* in which that concept is employed—and indeed it is possible for one individual to surpass another (or one generation to surpass another) in grasping and appropriating the logic of that concept simply by proceeding further in the direction of transcendence, towards which that logic points.

In discussing the transcendental, universal conception of God with both lay persons and individuals designated as theological experts, in the course of my teaching, lecturing and travelling, I have found that one issue arises recurrently—where are the power, the energy, the vitality, the life, the personality, which the popular imagination associates with the divine? The beginning of an answer to this question must arise from the recognition that there is no such thing as an expert on God. The absolute and transcendent perfection of God as understood in the integrated concept of divinity precludes the penetration of the human analytical intelligence, which is finite and can know nothing of the infinite save only its direction—symbolically represented as upward, that is toward perfection but transcending all humanly conceptualized and so delimited notions of the perfect.[26] It was the recognition of this fact which was expressed in the Mosaic iconoclasm, and it was the failure to recognize it which led to pagan charges of atheism against Jews in antiquity.

The Roman soldiers who penetrated the Holy of holies in Jerusalem swept the empty air with their spears seeking the unseen Jewish God. Pagan popular imagination filled the empty room with hideous abominations. From a pagan standpoint a god was not real that could not be seen, touched, felt, smelt, even tasted or cohabited with. The Jews were atheists, not only in their God's exclusivity but also in His incorporeality and His lack of the familiar determinations of objects. Even Spinoza's reassertion in modern terms of God's infinitude and transcendence of objecthood were taken by his contemporaries and by many since who should have known better as clear proof of atheism on his part. The tendency has persisted to this day to dismiss as "arid" or "unsuited to religious purposes" (as though religious purposes could go beyond intellectual adoration and ethical emulation without ceasing to be religious) any conception of divinity not bound to imaginative particularity, any insight toward Godhead founded upon natural rational religion or rational mysticism.

Philosophically such notions will not hold up. Any derogation from the Absolute is a derogation from the divine. Only the Absolute can be accorded recognition as divine—hence the Mosaic abomination of idolatry, which accords the due of the divine to values which are less than absolute. It is for this reason that in glossing the Biblical application of the notion of hatred to divinity, Maimonides argues that the metaphor of divine hatred, applied in the Torah exclusively to idolatry and related practices, denotes logical distance. Since God is infinite Perfection, his transcendence of particularity is absolute and the treatment of any lesser being or notion as divine is at the furthest remove, the ultimate extreme from truth.[27]

He knows God best, the Rambam argues,[28] who is best prepared on grounds of logic to negate the most of Him, from the realm of predicates applied in our common language. Which is to say, he knows God best who knows and can demonstrate that he knows Him least, who knows that only when the Sanctum is empty of all things and notions can it be most truly said to be the dwelling place of God. The disappointment professed by fideists and agnostics that such should be the outcome of natural theology is expressive of the still undissolved entanglement of their thoughts in the mythic level of religion, which depends on mental images—if not perhaps on a disingenuous hope that their readers' and hearers' minds at least have remained so entangled. The God Sputnik and Soyuz did not collide with in space is identical with the God too subtle to engage the Roman spears.

I am convinced that it is not because we are incapable of thinking conceptually that the true God eludes our grosser attempts to capture, bottle (or purvey!)—Him, for we think conceptually quite regularly in mathematics and even occasionally in the physical sciences. Rather, I suspect, we are unused to applying conceptual thought in the sphere of religion. The God we miss was the God of Sunday school and Bible tales, and we have not often enough aroused the mind to ponder on theology beyond the level of Sunday school images or to study the Bible as other than a collection of tales. It was in recognition of the potential of imagery to mislead, I think, that Maimonides advised parents from the earliest age (in marked contrast to Plato, who for practical purposes, was content that the belief of the commonalty should remain at the level of images) to inform their children that God is not a person or a thing.[29]

Hume, Bayle, Voltaire and the numberless intellectual flotsam which drifts in the currents set up by the fall of such giants from naive faith, were convinced that the God of true religion is the God of simple faith. Failing to find that God they believe that they (meaning religion) have failed absolutely. Their pose of melancholy loss is communicated to the Bertrand Russell's and Walter Lippmann's of the twentieth century with some loss of erudition, wit, and stylistic verve but no loss of the essential ingredient, a true Rousseauvian introspective (if not narcissistic) angst. The Fitzgerald *Rubaiyat,* a quintessential expression of what Voegelin calls "the Victorian fashion of agnosticism" encapsulates perfectly the course of such a spiritual autobiography:

> Myself when young did eagerly frequent
> Doctor and Saint and heard great Argument
> About it and about: but evermore
> Came out by the same door as in I went.[30]

To which the Sages answered long in advance: If you did not find, you did not seek. These men who weep for the lost God of their childhood seem rather to be mourning childhood, which indeed they will never recapture, rather than God.

Voltaire defines a theologian[31] as a man who has devoted many years

to the study of arcane languages and archaic civilizations in his quest for
God and still knows no more and may indeed know less than when he
began. Ibn Tufayl describes the learned seeker in much the same terms:
Absal has frequented the credos of all men before he learns that God is to
be encountered from the first in solitude. The motto Ghazali imparts to
his would be disciple (which Ibn Tufayl adopts) is this:

> Forget what you've heard and clutch what you see.
> At sunrise what use is Saturn to thee?[32]

Tradition can be an aid, but it may be a hindrance. There is in one way
more in common between sophisticated faith and disappointed atheism
than either the atheist or the traditionalist may realize. For once the glass
of naive faith is broken, as Ghazali put it, it can never be pasted together
or patched up but must be melted down and fused anew—or discarded.
The atheist and sophisticated believer both know that the God of naive
faith is not to be found. They differ only in their response—the atheist
complaining that the God of childhood or none is all that is worth
having; the pursuivant of natural religion, seeking a stronger, hardier,
higher and more mature conception of divinity. Thus the difference
between the two can often be expressed as a mere nuance of tone.
Plotinus, one of the greatest of the philosophic mystics, argues to the
conclusion that the prayer of the wise is silence. And for Thoreau
agnosticism becomes the triumphal motif through which the culmination
of the mystic search may be expressed: "Time is but the stream I go a-
fishing in. . . I know not the first letter of the alphabet."[33]

Childhood cannot be recaptured and we do not grow in human stature
in the attempt. Now we are men, we must seek with the eyes of men.

Personality cannot belong to God. For God is absolute, and personality is a confluence of biological exigencies with a potential for
divinity. As for the notions of energy, life, consciousness, power, these
are metaphors we assign to designate *actual* absolute Perfection by
reference to the relative perfections which we know. As applied to God
such terms are stripped of their familiar meanings. Since God is simplex,
they must be synonymous with one another and with Him. Since God is
transcendent and absolute they can have no reference to any common
experience whence we may have drawn them. This does not mean that
God is deprived of these or like "perfections" but only that He transcends the definitude they suggest. Compelled by the urgency of their
prophetic need to communicate the direction in which true divinity lies,
prophets by a kind of poetic license of their own (as Maimonides explained) apply to God these notions and that of personality—which

creates a dramatic theater for the expression of all sorts of values and ideas to which humans can relate. But to imagine we are *properly* describing the divine by such terms as these would be, as Rabbi Haninah put it, like praising a king who possessed millions in gold for having silver. Personality and the rest are notions from our world.

Spinoza, despite the survival of the ignorant notion that he denied divine transcendence, perhaps expressed this point best: consciousness and extended matter, since God is all, are two aspects of divinity of which we have some conception. But if God is all and the All is boundless, there are an infinitude of other attributes or aspects, each in itself infinite in its way (but not absolutely), of which we have not the slightest conception because they have nothing in common with us and are therefore totally outside our experience, an infinitude whose plurality— including the duality of matter and consciousness—is transcended at a level of which we have no ken.

The notion of divinity I have presented does not delimit God but is an attempt to suggest the idea of divine absoluteness. The fideistic or would-be traditionalistic endeavors to prevent the "stripping" from God of His traditional attributes and epithets do limit God by confining his conception within the bounds of human imagination. It will be understandable, then, why the conception of God I have been suggesting cannot arise from linguistic analysis of the ordinary kind.

Ordinary linguistic analysis is the analysis of the usages of ordinary language. But those usages are diverse, diffuse and (quite understandably) often mutually contradictory if not self-contradictory, reflecting and often overstating the numerous diverse aspects of experience. Proverbs, which are the canons of ordinary folk experience, are notoriously contradictory to one another. Folk wisdom consists in the intuitive grasp of principles which allow the application of one such maxim in a given situation to the exclusion of the others. From ordinary linguistic usage it is impossible to derive a single coherent concept of God, then. For when folk usage speaks of the divine, it does so invariably to a purpose defined within a context which application itself defines. The divine thereby becomes synonymous with the unknown or more specifically with whatever unknown features of existence may be thought of or spoken of in a given context as controlling human destiny or fortunes. It is this sort of notional and linguistic climate in which pagan religious sensibility first finds the context of its expression and from which it must draw its elements. But the dialectical refinement of that very sensibility leads, as the preceding discussion has been intended to show, to the development of a critical conception of divinity. The pitting of value against value (which the limited social contexts of ordinary usage specifically restrict) leads to the higher integration of values and the ultimate synthesis of all values in a single absolue summation of values, which synthesis is achieved (once integration has proceeded to the point of moralizing and cosmologizing values and of integrating morality and cosmology themselves under the concepts of justice and order) through the purgation of the objectively negative values from the value sphere and from the Deity.

Monotheism therefore inevitably goes hand in hand with critical theology, that is with a theology which examines rather than merely employs the concept of divinity, and so continuously refines its God concept in the direction which the logical content of that concept requires. By 'goes hand in hand with' I do not mean a relation of coextensivity. It is not the case that all monotheists are critical philosophers nor certainly that all critical philosophers are monotheists. But in every cultural setting in which monotheism is found there will be a critical philosophy of monotheism, whether express in conceptual discussions or latent in the dialectic of values which may be tacit in laws, in art, in rituals, in symbols or in other institutions and cultural manifestations—latent, but potentially express, through the reflective restlessness of intellectual activity, which is an inseparable part of the life of every culture. And in every culture where there is critical theology monotheism will arise.

The evidence we have looked at, therefore, is not what might be called ethnographic or even doxographical evidence, for to rely on such would only be to cull from an ocean of material expressions of every sort of notion which anyone may happen to hold *or to express* in regard to the divine. The result, if past surveys are any indication, would be a comprehensive typology of every sort of notion as to divinity, philosophical and non-philosophical. And even that would not be terribly revealing, for even in the most "primitive" societies individuals preserve the human capacity to think and operate at numerous diverse levels within numerous diverse contexts which are (in so far as the choice of category sets applied is concerned) of their own creation.[34]

I was surprised to learn while visiting with a traditional (not primitive!) Yemenite family in Israel that the *paterfamilias,* a builder by trade, was building himself a bomb shelter in his new home. I asked if he believed his shelter would withstand an atomic shock. The standard "modern" reply is, 'That depends how near.' My host responded with an iridescent[35] modern/ancient reply: "If that happens (God forbid!)—if they drop an atom bomb—the Holy One, blessed be He, will reach down and pluck it from the sky!" His knowledge of forces and stresses told him what the structure he was building could withstand. His traditional lore gave him a linguistic strategy to fall back on. Yet he knew that God is not a body. This iridescence is too complex and too shifting for analysis, as was that of the same man's wife when she spoke of the loss of one of the youngest of her twelve sons in the Yom Kippur War. Her words were the traditional formula, *'Adonay Dayan Emet'*—God is a truthful Judge. Her words seemed more a shield than an expression of her intensions. Her meaning remained within her eyes and heart, unexpressed by her words and unalterably beyond analysis.

The examples I have chosen from the arguments of Plato, Epicurus, Aristotle, Plotinus, Maimonides, Xenophanes, Spinoza and others were not chosen to show that these philosophers agree about what the concept of divinity means or should mean. Still less were they selected in an effort to reveal the meanings of that concept in the dialogue of faith and doubt. For in the iridescence of that dialogue the notion of divinity may mean anything or nothing. The examples I have chosen illustrate various phases in the resolution of the dialectic of the concept of divinity, and from them the outlines of a process may be picked out, as from the properly stained nuclei of cells the phases of cell division may be pieced together, one cell representing one phase of the process and others representing other phases. My paradigm examples tend to come from philosophers, for the working out of the various phases of the dialectic I am speaking of is a philosophic task, and that is so whether those who perform it are labelled philosophers or not, for it is the activity of refining a concept and rendering it coherent. Together the philosophers who have labored toward the refinement of the concept form a community of discourse. It was such a sense of community of discourse, I believe, that Eusebius was endeavoring to express when he referred to all the work of Greek philosophy as a *praeparatio evangelica* an evangelic or harbinger preparation for the Christian dispensation. And a similar expression of community is contained in the term *ahlu 'l-ḥaqq,* the adherents of the Truth *i.e.* God, who as the source and sum of all values is the source and sum of all truth (the juncture of reality and knowledge conceived as values), an expression which Muslim and Jewish philosophical writers in Arabic apply to monotheist thinkers of all traditions.

The historical basis of Christianity, of course, was not pure monotheism but a compromise with pagan archetypalism—even to the point of placing human sacrifice and the mythic/magic figure of the dying God once again in the center of the religious consciousness— although now applied, ironically enough, to the resolution of a moral/spiritual dilemma rather than to problems of pollution or fertility. Hence Paul's I resolve to know no philosophy but Christ crucified.

Within the dialectic of the concept of divinity in so far as that dialectic is responsive to the pragmatic needs of human beings there is an urgency to retain the divine within the range of human grasp and an anxiety lest transcendence render immanence impossible and thus the divine inaccessible. Hence (what I take to be the very self conscious) reversion to a finite and limited version of divinity in Christianity, the immanentism of the *hulûlîs* or incarnationist heretics of Shiite Islam, the philosophical immanentism of Stoic pantheism.

The whole issue of an epistemological problem as to the nature and existence of God is in effect laid at the door of monotheistic transcendentalism, with the claim that these problems would never have arisen had not God been sought too high. The demand is in effect that of the ancient Israelites to Aaron, "Up! Make us gods that will walk before us. . ." gods we can see and feel and touch. Give us the divine in the immediacy of our experience—and keep it there. Confronted by the popular insistence, Aaron could not survive without conforming his actions to the mob's expectation. He lacked the personal power to rebuke them and the words to inform them of the incoherency of their demand for a manufactured god. Only his irony informed them of this, and the force of that irony must have been lost on most. When the amulets and charms of wives, daughters and sons had been fused into a single lump and emerged, oracularly, as a calf, Aaron spoke, reminding the Israelites of the immediate origins of the object, "These are thy gods, Israel, who brought you up out of the land of Egypt." (*Exodus* 32:1-4, 8, 24) The epithet might be subrepted, but how could the people remain unaware of the disparity between the lump of fused gold about which they celebrated and the transcendent source of the power they had so recently experienced? Aaron knew, if those who confronted him did not, that despite their atavistic yearning toward immanentism, there would be for them no returning on the path by which they had come. Particularity would not prove adequate once they had experienced universality even only glimmeringly.

The problem with the immanentist sort of move is that it takes place after at least some of the absolute or infinite features of the logic of God have come to be recognized within a particular cultural setting—inevitably, since such reversions as these are dialectical responses or reactions to the logic of transcendence. But since the response does not occur in a naive cultural setting (as does the primitive or pagan expression of religious sensibility which it seeks, romantically, to recapture), the contradiction it involves is easily made explicit and is often self-contained. For now what is claimed to be human (among *hulûlîs*), to have suffered and died (among Christians), to be composed of matter (among Stoics) is the one and absolute Divinity, which is known by members of the culture and often by the rejectors of transcendence itself to be the absolute and infinite, therefore inevitably transcendent Deity. Hence the association of paradox with the historic manifestations and expressions of mysticism as a quest to contain the Absolute.

The Stoics simply absorb the contradiction, assigning both finite/physical and infinite/non-physical attributes to their deity, in oblivion of the fact that some features of the logic of their God-concept are militating against others, and thus unwittingly paving the way for Plotinus to re-purify their conception (by dematerializing it) and absorbing all that was affirmative in it in his own Platonic scheme. The *hulûlîs* too walk a tightrope of equivocations, endeavoring to speak of the Absolute in non-absolute terms or vice versa, making claims whose fallacy is obvious to their opponents and concealed only by the intensity of enthusiasm among their adherents, whether traditional or Western/romantic. As for the Christians, it was possible politically for Christian authorities to impose some significant measure of verbal conformity to the equivocation which identified the finite with the Infinite in the Nicaean creed. But, as Maimonides reminds us, a creed does not consist in formulae and cannot consist in contradictory formulations but only in the affirmation of what is understood.[36] Thus the intuitive repugnance of the Near Eastern Christians for the notion that God had died upon the cross could take expression in the study of formal logic— particularly the *Categories,* whose opening sentence is the exposure of the fallacy of equivocation. And the logic of the concept of divinity as Infinitude, which had been compromised but never denied by the enthusiasts (else-it had been bootless to equate the finite with the divine), could reassert itself despite Christotheism—both out of its ancient and traditional roots and out of the dynamism of its own logic. Origen could discover a kindred spirit in Philo. And the author of the *Divine Names* could find a guiding light to his own suspicions in the reasonings of Plotinus and at the same time steal a march on the episcopal politicians of the councils by claiming an authority which antedated and out-ranked theirs in discovering Biblical authority for his ideas and ascribing his own work to the Athenian convert of Paul, Dionysius the Areopagite.

The Divine, "Dionysius" concludes, can only be what transcends all being and knowledge, contains and is the source of all (true) values. If it is a matter of concern how we can reach so utterly transcendent a divinity (as the writer well knew it was), the answer can be expressed by explicating the mystery of prayer: We do not in prayer move the Deity, neither physically nor pathetically, for the Absolute has neither location nor emotion, but rather we strive upward ourselves, toward self-perfection of our spiritual natures as the Law exhorts us to strive toward perfection (on a human scale) of our ethical natures.[37] Thus the possibility of its compromise within an intellectual tradition no more derogates from the coherency of the concept of God than does the possibility of ignorance or confusion within a cultural community as to the rules implicit in the governance of that concept's use or of the ultimate end to which those rules inexorably direct its meaning. The concept itself is self-righting, and the speed with which this occurs is simply a measure of the energy and logical penetration of those who concern themselves with its significance and the freedom with which they may explore its potentialities.

---

1. "That which is blessed and immortal is undisturbed and is the cause of no disturbance to another. Thus it is not moved by anger or favor, for all such things are found only in the weak." Chief Doctrines 1.

2. *Republic* 377–385, *cf.* 364–365. It is in this former context that Plato coins the term 'theology', defining it in effect as the worthy account of the divine, that is the account worthy of the divine nature—which is to say the account which comports with the concept of the divine. The theological thrust of these and related passages in Plato is often overlooked by superficial readers who import a contemporary concern regarding censorship and "the freedom of art and artistic expression" into their reading, as though Plato's true concern were actually the regulation of poetic expression per se and as though (anachronistically) the art he speaks of were the "purely aesthetic" art of modern times. To the modern liberal sensibility it is easily overlooked that what Plato is demanding, *and effecting,* here is a theological revolution, that is a radical transformation in the conception we will have of God. He speaks, of course, not of public legislation but of the thoughts (here, of the divine) which the individual who is to pursue justice (and for the sake of the view of whom the model of the state as individual writ large is introduced) should entertain. It is characteristic of Plato that he should, by making whipping boys of "the poets," contrive to appear conservative or reactionary at one of the most revolutionary points in his philosophy; and characteristic of the way we tend to read philosophy that we should be so commonly taken in by his elemental ruse.

3. *Cf.* E. R. DODDS, *The Greeks and the Irrational,* "Agamemnon's Apology," Berkeley, 1951 (1964), pp. 3 ff.

4. RUDOLF OTTO, *The Idea of the Holy,* Chapter IV, Oxford, 1923, 1950 (1969), pp. 13 ff.

5. This non-articulation of the categoreal distinctness of distinguishable categories has been felicitously termed 'compactness' by ERIC VOEGELIN in his important study *Order and History.* "We move," he writes in regard to the mythic level of consciousness in the introduction to that study, "in a charmed community where everything that meets us has force and will and feelings, where animals and plants can be men and gods, where men can be divine and gods are kings, where the feathery morning sky is the falcon Horus and the sun and moon are his eyes, where the underground sameness of being is a conductor for magic currents of good or evil force that will subterraneously reach the superficially unreachable partner, where things are the same and not the same, and can change into each other." See Volume I, *Israel and Revelation,* Louisiana, 1956 (1976), p. 3. Compactness, I emphasize, does not merely "override the separateness of substances," but ignores or in its more sophisticated phases actively rejects the very notion of a necessary distinction between cause and effect, agent and patient, symbol and object, name and function.

6. Xenophanes is said to have rebuked Homer and Hesiod for their accounts of the gods (DIOGENES LAERTIUS *Lives of the Philosophers* IX 18). He wrote, "The Ethiopians say that their gods are snub-nosed and black, the Thracians that theirs have blue eyes and red hair." And, reducing the position, by analogy, to absurdity, he argued, "Why if cattle and horses or lions had hands, and were able to draw and do the things that men can do, horses would draw the forms of gods like horses, and cattle like cattle, and they would make their bodies such as they each had themselves," CLEMENT *Stromateis* VII 22, 1, V 109, 3; tr. after KIRK and RAVEN in *The Presocratic Philosophers,* Cambridge, 1957 (1962), pp. 168–169, items 171–172.

7. For Parmenides' discipleship of Xenophanes see DIOGENES LAERTIUS *Lives of the Philosophers* IX 21–23 and ARISTOTLE *Metaphysics* Alpha 5, 986b22. For his poetical expression of his mystical awakening and the dualism it established between truth and

illusion, SEXTUS EMPIRICUS, *Against the Logicians* I, III and SIMPLICIUS *De Caelo* 557.25. For the radical dichotomy of 'is' and 'is not,' PROCLUS' *Commentary on the Timaeus,* I 345; and the rejection of non-being/negation, SIMPLICIUS *Physics* 117.4, PLATO *Sophist* 237a and SEXTUS *Against the Logicians* I, 114. These and the remaining passages detailing the implications of Parmenides' monism are collected in KIRK and RAVEN, *The Presocratic Philosophers,* Cambridge, 1962.

For Aristotle's dismissal of the Eleatic equivocation, *Categories,* passim.

For the persistence in Megarian and Stoic thinking of Eleatic monism and insistence on overstrict interpretation of the exclusion principle, see SEXTUS *Against the Physicists* II 48, 85, 120, *Against the Professors* I 311. *Cf.* CICERO *De Divinatione* I lvi, 127, where the Stoic urges in behalf of determinism, "the passage of time is like the unwinding of a rope: it creates nothing new but only unfolds each event in its order." Like Eleatic monism, Stoic determinism (and many of its successors) is founded upon strict and global interpretation of the law of the excluded middle: a thing is what it is, hence must be what it is, cannot have been in any way other, ergo could not ever have been in any way other. Aristotle himself falls under the spell of this reasoning, at certain times and in some regards. Diodorus Cronus' arguments against the reality of motion are founded on the notion that each object is where it is. They thus make clear the nexus between Parmenides' logical rejection of variance and his pupil, Xeno's geometrical rejection. Motion requires that a thing "not be where it is" (we would say 'was') and so seems to militate against self-identity.

For Plato's "compromise," with negation see *Sophist* 254–260.

8. *Cf.* E. R. DODDS, *The Greeks and the Irrational,* "From Shame-Culture to Guilt-Culture." Berkeley, 1964, pp. 28–34.

9. One instance of a telling phase in the further ordering of divinity is outlined in F. M. CORNFORD'S masterful essay *From Religion to Philosophy,* London, 1912, New York, 1957 (1965); see especially pp. 13 ff.

10. *Cf.* ARTHUR DARBY NOCK, *Conversion,* Oxford, 1933 (1965), p. 12; ANDRÉ-JEAN FESTUGIÈRE, *Personal Religion Among the Greeks,* Berkeley, 1954 (1960), pp. 2, 20–21, 51, 105, 118: The *homoiosis theoi* of Plato, which provides the watchword of spiritual mysticism and theistic ethics springs from the divine assimilation of the pagan mysteries, as an interpretation of the primal mystic objective, the attainment of unity with (or subjective transference to) the divine.

11. See chiefly *Republic* VI-VII, 503–510 and following.

12. That Parmenides' efforts in behalf of conceptual integration were inconclusive is evident in the problematic relation of the Way of Truth to the Way of Seeming. Regardless of how modern thinkers may supply this missing nexus, their efforts will remain unsatisfactory from the Parmenidean viewpoint. For the object of Parmenides was to unify all reality as a single monadic Being and this required the negation of all "otherness," plurality and diversity, the denial of phenomenal multiplicity as illusion and the elimination of negation itself as a category, acts plainly contradictory to the ultimate unitive intent, since they *involved* the positing of a duality between reality and illusion and in some fashion the negating of the nether pole of that duality.

Whether Plato's efforts to resolve the problem in more qualified terms, accepting relative negation while rejecting absolute negation might ultimately have achieved his more modest goal remains in question until it can be clarified whether the relation of the One and the Indefinite Dyad can be described in non-mythical, conceptual terms. It is plain, however, that the neo-Platonists and Aristotelians, who sought to achieve such a goal by systematizing Plato and transforming much of his poetry into prose, rested so heavily on Plato's seminal recognition of the equivocal status of being in its finite manifestations as to call into question the seriousness and consistency of their commitment to formal logic, the Aristotelians treating matter both as Platonic "otherness" and as a kind of undefinable "thing," while the neo-Platonists and their followers made so much of the simultaneous identity and difference of the hypostases with one another as to render questionable the whole enterprise of crocheting ontologies out of the categories of logic.

As for the Stoics, their equivocations were not confined within a single region of their philosophic cosmos but extended to their notion of God (both active and passive, natural, extended, concentrated and divine), of nature (fiery, intelligent, providential, determined according to law), of matter (finite, seamless, moving, alive, animated by a self-nature which was at once supervenient, filling space, yet not excluding other matter from the same space), and, above all, of time (played out *in extenso* yet simultaneously omni-present and somehow, like all dimensions of multiplicity, ultimately unreal, its diversity at bottom illusory, and yet at once phenomenally real).

Monotheism does not, of course, resolve this set of problems, at least not to the satisfaction of the frame of reference which creates them. Like Plato it seeks unity in the divine and finds only the reflection of that unity in nature. But this goal, more modest than that of non-dualistic monism may be for that reason more attainable. Divine transcendence allows the world its categories. The key to such an approach is expressed symbolically in the old notion of kabbalistic theodicy that God restrained Himself with reference to creation, not seeking to pervade it but content rather to let it be as finite beings may be. The same idea is expressed in a more ontological metaphor by Kant: the condition of existence is freedom. (See *Lectures on Ethics, ad fin.*)

13. *Genesis* 18:25.

14. For LUCRETIUS (*De Rerum Natura* I 80–101) the sacrifice of Iphigenia at Aulis is paradigmatic of the (impious) works of religion—*"tantum religio potuit suadere malorum."* The force of moral argument is brought to bear against the wicked power of religion. But his represents an advanced phase of thinking on the subject of religion, presupposing a consensual moral consciousness which is differentiated from the value notions articulated under the guise of divinities. For the Homeric consciousness if one value were to be delimited, *i.e.* one god's acts subjected to criticism, it would have to be by another—Poseidon pressing his claims against those of Zeus. The capability of questioning the divine and so refining its conception presupposes a disentanglement of value concepts from the prevailing positive notions of divinity which goes beyond the pitting of one god against another and requires in some measure the appropriation of those concepts by consciousness to itself.

15. Indeed we learn from Vergil and from the sort of evidence collected by FRAZER in regard to the cult of John Barleycorn that even the violation of a plant might be fraught with the same significance—that from the wounds inflicted on a tree or on a stand of grain groans might issue and divine or magic forces issue forth.

16. See PORPHYRY *On Abstinence from Animal Food* II. As for the ritual significance of every meal according to Mishnah (*Avot* 3:4): "Rabbi Simeon says, 'If three have eaten at one table and not spoken words of Torah over it, it is as though they had eaten the slaughtered victims of the dead; as it is said "All tables are filled with vomit and filth without the All-inclusive." But if three have eaten at one table and spoken over it words of Torah, it is as though they had eaten at the table of the All-inclusive, as it is written, "It was said to me, 'This is the table that is before God.' " ' " Hertz mistakes the brunt of the remark as mere rhetorical exaggeration. The point hinges on the contrast of the two texts: *Isaiah* 28:6, which asserts that *all* tables are filled with vomit and filth *and there is no clean place,* and the contrasting passage (*Ezekiel* 41:22) which describes one table as that of the Lord. Clearly that table is not defiled. How then are we to understand Isaiah's universal condemnation? Plainly he refers (as the context shows) to all tables at which the spirit of God *(Shechinah)* was not invoked. So Simeon translates *'beli makom'* not as 'and there is no clean place' but as 'without the All-inclusive,' taking *makom* in its rabbinic sense as a designation of God. And it is in accordance with this construction that R. Simeon glosses, assuming in agreement with R. Chananya (*Avot* 3:3) that discussion of Torah is the appropriate means of invoking the *Shechinah.* But in the absence of such invocation, there is a presumption of its negation—hence, *all* tables. This presumption might have been read as a supposition that pagan gods lurk unless the *Shechinah* has been invoked to dispel them, but Simeon is careful to say 'sacrificial victims of the dead' rather than 'of pagan gods,' lest he suggest a belief in the reality and omnipresence of the latter. The dead here are the inarticulate, non-living or non-real principles or values worshipped in pagan religions. Since a meal is a sacrament, R. Simeon argues, the failure to dedicate it to the All-inclusive implies its dedication (by negligent intent) to lifeless corpses, the values and principles falsely personified and deified, whose adoration is defilement. Crucially, there is no secular meal but only sanctification or desecration of the divine.

17. The goddess Artemis is for this reason not a minor diety.

> . . . flying after her arrows flown down some
> tremendous valley-side . . .
> Chasing the mountain goats or ghosting deer . . .
> taller by a head than nymphs can be
> the goddess shows more stately, all being beautiful . . .
>   (*Odyssey* VI 103 ff. tr
>   Robert Fitzgerald, Garden City,
>   1961.)

She captures, crystalizes, personifies and transcends the elemental experience in which she is discovered, and is, I fear, still sought. The terror of the goddess stems from the fact that the frisson in which she is discovered is that of death. Thus her arrows are the plague and what she demands is death, service to the value she expresses.

18. Kierkegaard's famous meditation on the *Akedah* or binding of Isaac wholly misses the point of the Biblical narrative by projecting onto it an anachronistic Protestant notion of the nature and role of faith and an equally anchronistic presumption of the patness of moral judgments. Faith for Kierkegaard is supposed to afford the sole ultimate salvation to man, for morality is meant to recognize its own futility in confrontation with sin and the inadequacy of repentence and so yield to pure faith. The ultimate test of faith, then, becomes the arbitrary demand that it part company (as though its content were to be arbitrarily selected or imposed) with morality. This is the celebrated teleological suspension of the ethical, which Kierkegaard pastes over the Biblical narrative as the best that he can bring to it.

But where does Abraham concern himself with sin? Where textually does he enunciate Kierkegaard's scruples as to the inadequacy of repentence? Where does he experience anguish over "faith" which Kierkegaard projects upon him? Even the word translated as 'faith' by Christian Bible readers and others who have come under the influence of Christian theology does not in general refer to faith in the Hebrew Bible—at least not in the sense that Augustine forged by merging Plato's *pistis* with Cicero's *fides*. It refers rather to stedfastness and loyalty. It is a moral/political term not a cognitive/volitional one and surely not a form of knowledge or a substitute for knowledge. The notion of justification by faith is as absent from the Torah as is that of cognition by faith or the preoccupation with justification (in Christian sense) altogether—for that presumes a judgment as to the inadequacy of life on earth and an expectation of its replacement with something better, could we but merit it—a family of notions wholly foreign to the values of the Torah and indeed contradicted by them.

So blinded is Kierkegaard by his personal struggle that he reads a kind of academic Kantian morality into Abraham's mind and then projects his own (rather pagan) notion of the possible or inevitable conflict of the Absolute divinity with that (human) morality at the very moment where the Biblical story represents the awakening of human consciousness to the indissolubility of true morality from the true conception of the Absolute.

19. *The Savage Mind,* Chicago, 1966 (Paris, 1962), p. 32.

20. *Cf. Deuteronomy* 12:31, where again, as is the Torah's mode, incompatibility within the bounds of moral logic is expressed as emotive abhorrence.

21. For further elaboration of this principle see my articles in *Judaism,* July, 1976, and *The Jewish Law Annual,* inaugural number, 1978, as well as the third of these lectures.

22. For some further reflections on this moral polarization of the cosmos see my introductory essay to my translation from the Arabic of *The Case of the Animals vs. Man Before the King of the Jinn,* "The Ecology of the Ikhwân al-Safâ'," Boston, 1978.

23. Some scholars have made much of the fact that one Hebrew word regularly employed to refer to God is apparently plural in grammatical form, even going so far as to translate it as a plural, "the gods." This neglects the fact that the verbs of which that term is the subject, created, called, etc. are regularly singular in form, so the word must have been construed as a singular when the sentences containing it were composed. Even etymological plurality is absent. For unlike the Hebrew words *mayyim, hayyim, shamayim,*

panim, water, life, heavens, and face, which are morphologically and etymologically plural (or dual) and take a plural verb (although often logically singular), *elohim* takes a singular verb. There is a singular form, *eloha,* which means god, but this is employed generically.

24. In *From Religion to Philosophy,* Cambridge, 1912 (repr. New York, 1965).

25. Hence the sense Maimonides gives to *Isaiah* 26:2: "Open ye the gates that the righteous nation that keepeth faith may enter," in superscribing it to his own essay on the logic of the concept of God, the opening chapters of the *Guide to the Perplexed.*

26. Thus the Hebrew *'yoshev bameromim'*—which does not denote a spatial direction.

27. See *Moreh Nevukhim* I 36, *cf.* I 18, 24; *cf.* IBN TUFAYL'S treatment of damnation as alienation from God, *Hayy Ibn Yaqzan,* p. 153 of my translation; *cf. Isaiah* 59:2.

28. *Moreh* I 52 ff.; see the texts and discussions in my *RAMBAM,* Part I.

29. *Moreh* I 35.

30. *Rubaiyat* 27, fifth ed., 1889. VOEGELIN'S remark is from the preface of his *Israel and Revelation,* 1956 (1976), p. xii.

31. In the *Philosophical Dictionary,* see Peter Gay's translation, New York, 1962, p. 480.

32. Ghazali's distych is from the *Munqidh min al-Dalâl* translated by William Montgomery Watt in *The Faith and Practice of al-Ghazali,* London, 1953 (1963). The present translation is my own, from its citation in Ibn Tufayl's *Hayy Ibn Yaqzan,* New York, 1972, p. 101.

33. *Walden,* New York, 1950 (first ed. 1854), p. 88.

34. For extensive argument and evidence in behalf of this claim, see Paul Radin, *Primitive Man as Philosopher,* New York, 1956 (expanded from the original ed. of 1927).

35. For the concept of iridescence I am indebted to a lecture by J. N. Findlay given at the international philosophical meetings in New York, March, 1976.

36. *Moreh* I 50.

37. *The Divine Names* III; 3, tr. C. E. Rolt, London, 1975 (1920, 1940), pp. 81–82, 86.

II

THE EXISTENCE OF GOD

By God we understand an absolute or infinite being, a being of infinite perfection, as it has sometimes been expressed, or a being who *is* infinite perfection and in relation to which all finite perfection is comprehended. This is not the folk concept of God or the mythic concept, but it is the inevitable ultimate outcome of the dialectical examination of the concept of divinity, and so it is the concept with which philosophers who inquire into theism must work, assuming that an object of their inquiries is a clarified and coherent idea of divinity.

The question which arises when this concept has been elucidated is whether or not such a being exists. It is natural for such a question to arise. Children ask a similar question when they reach the age of reason as to any traditional notions of divinity which they may encounter. And though adult responses to this sort of question (whether intended as affirmative or negative) may often have the effect of inculcating an evasive or hypocritical approach, cloaking or dismissing or shifting the issue rather than confronting it, it is a legitimate question and one which properly requires an answer.

The logical positivists, like their ancient forebears the Pyrrhonists, believed no question could be properly formulated unless there were specifiable means by which its answer could be determined—means whose range both these schools (and others of the same philosophical bent) were inclined to confine to a familiar realm of ordinary experience and (in the case of the logical positivists) simple logical reasoning. Unless sense perception or pure deductive reasoning (or some combination of the two) could suffice to settle a question, the question was assumed to be no real question and all proposed answers to it were held to be meaningless.

But it has long been recognized that an absolute being cannot be confronted *as such* perceptually,[1] and that deductive arguments must be regarded as deriving their certainty from the postulation of their premises and hence can establish no matters of fact, since any conclusion they reach is only the working out of the consequences of what they assume. It appeared to the positivists, therefore, that any attempted answers to the question about the existence of God were to be classified as non-propositions or nonsense, as it was put—beautiful, poetic nonsense, it was sometimes conceded, useful perhaps in some contexts and dangerous in others, but nonsense nonetheless, in any context.

It has been allowed, to be sure, by linguistic analysts of pluralistic stamp, that there are many more things to be done with language than the utterance of truths—interjections, expletives, oaths, promises, curses, wishes, professions of love or hatred, commands and prohibitions, among others, all have their places among the repertoire of linguistic strategies rendered canonical by those who take it as their mission to chart the logic of linguistic forms. And some adherents of religious traditions have happily seized upon these concessions, which accord scientific recognition to what they, as religionists knew, or suspected or hoped all along, as though the fact that a particular mode of discourse had been subject to scientific inquiry and formal analysis were somehow necessary or sufficient to establish the legitimacy of its use. But if by propositions were to be meant those sentential compounds which make a claim about the nature of things, which assert that such is so and imply that the alternatives are not, the fact remains that those thinkers who came within the orbit of logical positivist influence denied to the purported assertion of the existence of God any significance by the standard they described as necessarily applying to all such propositions.

Propositions which make truth claims, it was asserted, must have a truth value, true or false. And, it was implied, for this to be so that truth value must be, if not determinate at least determinable. There were, moreover, strict rules by which (and by which alone) such determination was to be achieved, rules derived from those in accordance with which the model enterprises of natural science and mathematics were assumed to be conducted. If the assertion of the existence of God could not pass muster by the same standards which were thought to have made possible such successes as quantum physics, and subsequently the H-bomb, it was assumed that the assertion had no significance (at least not of a propositional/descriptive sort) at all.

The possibility of taking such a stance as this regarding the question as to the existence of God rests upon the assumption that two realms of utterances can be clearly distinguished: propositions which are testable by empirical (*i.e.* perceptual) verification and those which are demonstrable within the framework of some deductive system. The possibility of dismissing statements about God's existence as metaphysics on grounds that they are unverifiable rests upon the possibility of assuming that within a realm of "commonsense," that is of sense perception and simple reasoning, verification (as positivistically conceived) *is* possible—otherwise, why single out particular classes of propositions for special treatment as "metaphysical." But the real chances of establishing the wished for realm of commonsense verification have always dimmed considerably when the notion has been subjected to philosophic scrutiny.

"Commonsense," for example, cannot establish through sense perception the real existence of any object outside of (*i.e.*, independent of) personal consciousness—neither bodies nor other minds, nor even (if it be confined strictly to sense perception and not allowed self-consciousness or self-intuition) the existence of one's own mind. This is not just a matter of the lack of certainty or weakness of evidence. Without a metaphysical assumption as to the nexus of sensory phenomena with reality, there is no evidence whatever to count in favor of or against the existence of anything beyond a single consciousness[2] or even to allow that consciousness itself to be asserted to be in any way entitative.

Phenomenalists, of course, especially since the times of Hume and Kant, have busied themselves with redefining bodies, minds, causes, etc. as figments of consciousness (one cannot say mine, since solipsism is surpassed in pure phenomenalism, my own self dissolving with all others on the Humean grounds that I do not perceive it in the same way that I imagine myself to perceive objects[3]). But all this redefinition, designed to bring some favored class of objects at least nominally back within the realm of verifiability, achieves nothing with regard to external objects, Kant's things in themselves (that is objects considered as real without reference to any sensory intuition of them). They remain at large, unverified and unverifiable (by these strict means), with no evidence accountable in their favor or against them. Their status, therefore, differs in no way epistemically from that of God, on this verificationist account. In point of verification by means of sense perception there is no difference to be made between God and any object which in any way lies or may lie outside my consciousness. The dismissal of inquiry about divine existence on the professed grounds of unverifiability is, therefore, specious. For the "commonsense" sensory realm of transcendental entities, with which sentences about God are contrasted, is itself an *ad hoc* fabrication, for which, when verificationism is consistently applied, a phenomenal (non-transcendental) realm is substituted.

Some philosophers believe that the maintenance of discourse on a purely phenomenal basis is impossible. Language, they argue, or thought, presupposes a community of discourse. Both Wittgenstein and Heidegger argue in this vein in their separate ways. But this line of argumentation has something of a magical aura about it, as though the combination of wish and need, two parts myth and three parts pragmatism could assure us that what we require is (lo and behold!) already ours. There is no other realm of discourse, it seems to me, besides this metaphysical one, in which the fact that we presume a fact or relation or some other object of desire is taken as warranting the veracity of our presumption. And metaphysics seems a poor place to introduce such a method. The claim that we presume a thing to be so, and so it must be, is simply fallacious, circular, not a consideration well enough anchored epistemologically to afford purchase for the erection of an ontology. We can no more conclude the reality of other minds because our language presumes them than we can conclude the reality transcendental things because our language presumes them.

The assumption of a formal incoherency in phenomenalism, moreover, has been shown to be false in a practical way. The work of phenomenalistic philosophers from Sextus to Russell, Ayer and Phillipp Frank is fairly convincing testimony to the possibility of elaborating a comprehensive transformation system by which statements which do presume an objective, transcendental correlative might be exchanged for others which do not. Ordinary language, in such a scheme, would be regarded (once its inevitable confusions had been purged) as employing in its idioms a system of useful fictions such as that of causality, that of external objects, that of the entitative self, etc. On these conditions such idioms could continue in use, provided that the means of their unpacking into the presumptively verifiable elements which afford their "cash value" can be kept ready at hand. Every transcendental judgment would be prefixed by a formal reservation: "as if," or "seemingly"—paralleled and parodied by the practice of the so-called beat generation of the '50's preceding all judgments with the word 'like.' By such means the transcendental presumptions of language can in principle be purged. Yet the material terms and formal relations of language would remain explicitly transcendental, preserving a dependence on a realm of entities no longer explicitly held to be real. Herein lies the weakness of the phenomenal reduction. In the circumstances where the reduction is most complete and systematic it becomes dubious which is the fiction, the entitative assumptions of language/thought or the notion that these have been replaced or rendered otiose.

The problem is not with the adequacy of the reductive transformation rules to transpose (in principle) all entitative, causal, etc. statements to phenomenal statements which may be regarded as their formal

THE EXISTENCE OF GOD 39

equivalents (although explicitly they refer to materially different states of affairs) but rather in the constant reliance of the products of this reductive analysis for their material terms and the formal structures and relationships they incorporate, and from which they derive their differentiated content, upon the unreduced notions of the unanalyzed (or "pre-critical") levels of discourse. Since the reductive language is systematically parasitic upon that "naive" language, and is so essentially if even the formal correspondence of analysans to analysandum is to be maintained (rather than the analysis merely degenerating into a mass of unstructured and undifferentiated data), it becomes questionable whether the analysis has moved at all closer to the elemental. It is here that the primitive categories of "naive" experience—substance, quality, cause, things, mind, etc.—seem most to assert their vitality or resistance to reduction. There is a sense, then, in which phenomenalism does not seem likely to achieve success in its aim of removing all metaphysical presumptions from human (thought and ?) language.

But regardless of the fruitfulness or sterility of phenomenal reductivism as an ontological strategy, the fact remains that on verificationist assumptions no epistemic distinction can be drawn between statements about God and other statements as to the existence of any other non-subjective being or state of affairs. If objective statements are exclusively objective and remain so, then subjective judgments cannot verify them. If their verifiability is to be assured by their subjective reduction (so that they can participate in the certainty and self-containedness of the subjective state), then they are robbed of their objective sense. The same is true of all purported claims of objective fact regardless of their subject matter.

So the claim that answers to the question as to God's existence are nonsense because of the alleged absence of a clear perceptual standard of verification such as would be used (purportedly) in verifying ordinary statements of fact falls to the ground. Verificationism strictly applied allows no such statements of fact unless they are reducible to reports of sense data and robbed of all transcendental or objective import. Thus, through a strictly sensuous empiricism, statements of fact are preserved as possible but only as subjective, not as objective facts, that is only at the cost of reversion to a Protagorean identification of truth with seeming.

Even when this step has been taken, for the sake of verifiability, verification of quite non-theological judgments remains problematic at best. For now, verification consists in specifying the sensory phenomena for which a speciously objective judgment stands as surrogate. But if that is the case it is impossible to see how verification will verify. The naive judgment, 'I see a cow' is naively verified by appropriate sensory phenomena. But, on the phenomenalist analysis, 'I see a cow' has no external reference. It refers only to those same phenomena. The verification of it, then, is specious, being achieved only by repetition of what now must be regarded as an identical judgment.

So long as the distinction is preserved between reality and appearance there will be no distinction to be made in point of verification through the senses between assertions or denials of the existence of God and assertions or denials regarding any other transcendental objects, entities or events such as bodies, causes, others' selves or our own. It is thus that the claim that attempted answers to the question about God's existence are meaningless on grounds that they do not conform to the "usual" standards of verification through the senses fails. For no judgments as to any transcendental entities, or any causes or even our own minds are possible by the criteria proposed. And if our notions of meaning are adjusted to accommodate verification by the admission of systematic phenomenalist reduction as in principle an appropriate mode of translation, the only result is to trivialize the notion of verification itself by equating that which is to be verified with its means of verification.

As for the analytic type of statement, it must be noted first that the distinction of analytic or formal judgments from factual or material judgments is not an absolute but a relative one. The postulates of any consistent system related to nature or experience may be posited as a mathematical system, and within that system all valid deductions from those postulates must be treated as analytic. Whether it is possible to create a purely formal system, such as mathematics has at times been represented to be, is very much in doubt—to put the matter civilly, for that doubt is in fact diminished to indubitable impossibility (if the system is to be thought by human beings) by the recognition that all human thought is discursive and thus timebound.

It was Descartes who taught us, in effect, that all judgments, since they involve time, the movement of the mind from subject to predicate or, as in mathematics from one term to another of a relation, are synthetic. He expressed this fact dramatically by the inclusion of mathematical judgments within the realm in which error is possible, deception, illusion, the subreption in the mind of one term in place of another, systematic deception by a superior intelligence or the conceivably undetectable deception of the mind by an omnipotent, malevolent agent. Wherever there is movement there is the logical possibility of slippage. Whenever thought moves, it may mistake its object. It is for this reason, I take it, that Descartes chose intuitions (self-consciousness, the idea of Perfection, etc.) rather than propositions as the foundations of his reconstructed knowledge. And Plato expressed a parallel insight when he alluded to the highest forms of knowledge as rational intuitions (of the forms) and referred to the sort of propositional system of theorems which we call science, as a "likely story." As soon as knowledge entrusts itself to the propositional level it becomes synthetic, because it pieces together (or, as Aristotle expressed it, interweaves) one notion with another, and so becomes subject to sound and faulty combination, the possibility of error.

When Kant argued *in effect* that all judgments are synthetic, even those like '5 + 7 = 12,' which we often feel inclined to call analytic, it was this fact that he was recognizing. Relying on the subject-predicate format and Leibniz' account of analyticity (by which a proposition is analytic if the concept of its predicate is contained within that of its subject), Kant argued that given the concept of addition and those of 5 and 7, 12 goes beyond those concepts. This givenness, Kant assumed, is a mental event. If there were some Platonic or Carnapian realm in which "mathematicals" might subsist eternally and possess eternal relations among themselves, relations which need not be humanly thought, then we could speak, perhaps by reference to that realm, of the predicate of this judgment as containing no more than does its subject—that is if we could be assured somehow as to the adequacy of our notions of the realities of that realm. But even if the reality of such a realm is assumed, that metaphysical assumption need hardly be comprised within our notions of particular numbers. Staying strictly within the confines of the content of our ideas, if we know nothing of 12, then '5,' '+,' '7' and '=' will not yield it for us.

Consider a budget-model calculator containing just one place for formulation and display of solutions to addition problems. It contains the digits 0–9 and numerals for their display but not 10 or any higher number. It has a logic comparable to that which Pascal used in programming the first wooden digital calculator for his father. That is to say, it can add. But it has no 12; or, speaking psychologically, no notion of 12. Now enter 5, add 7. No 12 can appear. The display may read out 9 or 0 or 1, or 2 or E for error, depending on the convention which has been allowed for such eventualities, but there simply is no 12. The judgment '5 + 7 = 12' is synthetic in that conceptually 12 goes beyond just 5 + 7, as is obvious when it is considered that 12 is also 6 + 6 and 72 ÷ 6 and so *ad infinitum;* or psychologically, by the fact that when I think of 5 and 7 and adding, I need have no thought of 12, or if perhaps I am a small child, no notion of it as yet. The whole matter is psychological—as it must be if these things (numbers) are not assumed to exist in and of themselves.

Of course in some neatly-formed and eternal conceptual system, we may be told, '6 + 6' and '5 + 7' are one and the same entity. We may be given grounds for distinguishing sense from reference, denotation from connotation. But then it may be objected, after Kant, that such a system, if it does exist, must be in someone's mind, and it is there that the identifying synthesis has been made. Even if it be conceded that somehow there subsists a Platonic-Carnapian realm where eternal truths are true and the diversity of 5 + 7 and 6 + 6 is not merely synthesized but dissolved into ontic unity, the fact remains that *that* realm is not contained within the far less imposing notions constituting '5 + 7 = . . .' in such a manner that this alone can yield 12, or any answer, in abstraction from some context of relations or conventions by which an answer might be arrived at and revealed.

That all judgments (including those we call by courtesy analytic in view of some system of postulates or conventions we have presupposed and choose in that case to invoke) are, whatever else they may be, synthetic is obvious from the form of judgment, which is complex and thus involves the unification of elements. Kant relied upon the subject predicate form of statement: A judgment synthesizes by affirming a predicate of a subject. No judgment can be strictly analytic, for in some way every predicate must go beyond the notion of its subject if only in order to be predicated of it. More broadly we may think of relational propositions (a type which Leibniz banned for failing to meet the conditions of his analysis); but the fact remains—there is still a synthesis of elements. Even in a statement of identity we have more in the "predicate" than 'what is contained in the concept of the subject,' for there is an operator of predication (or relation) to which convention assigns a role as expressing identity or equating, and then the subject term again but now repeated and so not identical as at its first occurrence. Its syntactical role is altered, as it must be if it is to complement the subject and complete the judgment rather than simply beginning another. So every proposition is synthetic, in that it combines elements, although some may be analytic in regard to the adequacy of their subjects to the implication of their predicates—*provided* sufficient postulates, definitions and conventions have been presumed to allow such implication to proceed.

But if all judgments, being compounds or complexes, are synthetic, we must heed what the medieval theologians tell us, that what is combined need not have been so—at all or in the manner that we find it. Hence all judgments involve contingency.

Judgment is possible, moreover as Kant recognized, only through synthesis not only of its terms but of the manifold of phenomena in time, which otherwise would negate or obviate the unity of consciousness, in which those terms and phenomena are brought together. Here again, if synthetic always, judgment is fallible always, contingent always. The ultimate contingency of all discursive thinking is the foundation of the validity of the claim made by Quine in his famous essay, "Two Dogmas of Empiricism," that we have no grounds by which to place our so-called analytic propositions at an absolute remove from all the rest of understanding but rather must assume that there may be circumstances under which even the most sacrosanct and seemingly self-evident of our analytic judgments might have to be called into question, revised or discarded.[4]

Recognizing the contingency of all human judgments, which arises from the very character of discursive thinking, and assuming that this was a reflection of some ontic instability in their subject matter, the medieval theologians, schooled by Plato, relied upon the presumption that human awareness of God, in whom as an absolutely perfect Being there is no instability, must be non-discursive, that is intuitive, meaning, technically speaking, outside time, and thus transcendent of the ordinary conditions of ordinary human consciousness, that is ecstatic—not a surprising conclusion, in view of the elevation of the Subject said to be apprehended, but a highly problematic one from the perspective of ordinary human psychology and phenomenology. For in ordinary human experience time is never transcended, and by the canons of that experience it seems impossible to conceive how it could be. Thus a sort of warfare ensued between the canons of ordinary experience, which are wont to call themselves logic (although they contain no self-evident and inevitable criterion of certainty as to matters of fact) and those of mystic ecstasy, which is wont to call itself a higher truth, each experience calling the other incoherent, fleeting, fragmentary and dubious and claiming to possess some higher or drier ground from which the other might be judged—a conflict which has long resulted in confusion (both on the part of mystics and on that of their detractors) fairly widespread, between mysticism and mystagoguery or obscurantism and (both on the part of advocates of the ordinariness of "ordinary" experience and *their* detractors) of science and logic with sterility or nihilism.

I profess to have no privileged standpoint from which to judge the contents or the canons of one mode of experience against another but confess that I have none and that I would regard as suspect any utterance which purported to express such a higher standpoint, for I see no means by which any human judgment may be vindicated as true by anything contained solely within itself or any experience warranted to reveal what it appears to reveal solely by elements contained within itself. I do not pretend that like the fellow in the eastern dream I have no notion whether I am a man dreaming myself a butterfly or a butterfly dreaming myself a man. Nor do I pretend that I do not know whether it is better to be awake or dream or sleep dreamlessly. I claim only that I have no evidence and can conceive of none which would without circularity or question begging establish the credentials of ecstasy to sit in judgment upon any other dimension of experience or any which on the same terms would establish the possibility of ecstasy being judged by other modes of awareness.

This is not to say that each mode of experience is inviolate and in *that* way infallible. For each can be judged internally by standards which arise from a dialectic of its own. Nor is any mode of experience impenetrable to the rest. The limitations of each may be criticized by all, but the findings in such a case, when a mode of experience is judged by standards extrinsic to its own, will not always be relevant to the matter of the first. William James found fascinating correlations between ecstasy and certain varieties of dementia[5], but this has no particular bearing on the worth or worthlessness of some prophet or saint or visionary's insight or message, just as the moral condemnation a prophet might wish to heap upon, say, a particular scientist has no special bearing on the truth or falsity of any scientific hypothesis that investigator may moot. It may be true (but need not be) that researcher A would be a better man or even a better scientist if he knew some moral or spiritual truths or at least if he did not ignore or thwart the side of his nature from which insight into such regions might grow. Or it may be that mystic B would be a saner man, perhaps a more effective prophet, more insightful spiritualist or sage were he to undergo some course of self-analysis or to know more of astronomy. But neither of these possibilities has much to do with the value or valuelessness of the discoveries made by A or B using the method each knows best. Any approach may be judged by standards extrinsic to its own, but it can hardly be expected that such judgments will correspond invariably with those made by other standards or even deal with the same subject matter. There is, then, no means by which one mode of material discourse can rule another absurd, impossible or incomprehensible.

Rhetorically, logic has been the bastion of the defenders of ordinary discourse against the kind of extraordinary discourse which is required if one is to speak at all anent a perfect Being. But logic forbids only self-contradiction, that is the contradiction of what has already been posited or understood. In such a case either the former understanding or the latter if not both must be modified or abandoned. But except in such a case logic contributes nothing. It makes clear only the possible incompatibility of one conception or preconception with another. Moreover, the ability to distinguish a clear-cut realm of logical propositions which can be demonstrated by deductive reduction to certainties (*i.e.*, axioms and statements of identity), which has been the ideal of mathematics ever since Euclid created the first (more or less) self-contained and (more or less) rigorous deductive system, has been (again to put the matter civilly) called very much into question by the work of Gödel in the present century.

Gödel demonstrated[6] that in any formal system sophisticated enough to allow the generation of number theory (*e.g.,* any system such as that of Russell and Whitehead in their *Principia Mathematica*) there will be some formula (true in that system) whose affirmation and negation are not provable by deductive resort to the axioms of that system. This means that all such systems are formally incomplete, that regardless of how their axiom sets are constituted or supplemented, some (true) proposition, formulated in the terms of any such system will inevitably remain undecidable by deductive reduction to the axioms of that system. This does not mean, of course, that mathematics falls in a heap to the ground, that deduction is impossible or the deductive method fruitless. It does not even mean that the formally undecidable propositions Gödel conceived are absolutely undecidable. As mathematical intuitionists are fond of pointing out, they are informally decidable. But Gödel's theorem (along with its proof) does show that the notion of mathematical verification by deductive reduction to axioms, upon which the logical positivist idea of verification was founded is inadequate. For true and intuitively evident propositions are formulable within any mathematical system which can generate an arithmetic, which yet are not demonstrable, hence not verifiable within that system.

Further, strict positivistic demonstration involves reduction not to axioms but to certainties. It is by no means clear since the development of non-Euclidean geometries, whether any mathematical axiom can be regarded as self-evidently certain, or even (in view of the degree of arbitrariness with which axiom systems may be constituted) whether the notion of truth should continue to be applied in mathematics. For the logical positivists, mathematical certainty tends to be ascribed in the first instance to identity statements, and only secondarily to axioms and other mathematical judgments, although there is a tendency to refer to these as well, the axioms and theorems of mathematical logic, as tautologies when the speaker wishes to emphasize their derivation from or reducibility to identity statements or to emphasize their non-empirical character. But to proceed from an identity statement to an axiom (if this can be done) involves a synthesis, as it does to proceed from a set of axioms to a theorem or theorems. And even an identity statement, as we have seen, is synthetic, since such a statement posits a relation of identity and does not merely stand pat with the given. The tautology 'A is A,' viewed as a judgment (and not as an eternal verity descended miraculously from a Platonic realm of timeless truth without somehow losing its timelessness) involves a synthesis of notions and a unification over the manifold of time.

But even if it be granted that identity statements, tautologies in the strict sense, are certainties, and their synthetic character as manifolds both in logical structure and in psychological nature (as processes) is forgotten, the derivation of more complex statements from them remains problematic. It involves the erection of a complex axiom system sophisticated enough to generate from identity statements other judgments of far greater complexity. And with each subsequent step towards complexity the pure equivalency of the given with what is to be derived from it is left further behind. At no point was there a trivial identity in objective terms of the premise-set with the conclusions to be predicated upon it, for such identification always contained subjectivity and process among its elements; and as the elaboration of the system proceeds, with all its ramifications, the contingency introduced by the fact that the whole is a subjective system, apprehended if not created by human intelligence, increases, not in kind but in degree.

Because all judgments are synthetic, then, and because not all mathematical judgments are deductively verifiable in the formal systems from which they are drawn, the notion that meaning depends on verification as understood by logical positivists falls to the ground. For strict empirical verification of matters of fact turns out to be possible only if those matters of fact are themselves reduced to the very sense data by which they are to be verified and the relation of verification is then trivialized into the expression of equivalence between phenomenologically reduced statements and the phenomena which are claimed now to be both their contents and their proof; and mathematical verification turns out to be possible only if it is assumed that we can have access to an objective realm where true theorems are equivalent to axioms and axioms to tautologies—and even if it is assumed that this is so, Gödel's work shows that it is not so in every case.

The question, then, of whether God exists is not to be distinguished radically from other questions in point of verification as positivistically understood. For it is not clear that any of our ordinary propositions regarding any transcendental objects we believe or understand ourselves to encounter are verifiable or refutable, confirmable or disconfirmable (since what has no bearing can neither add weight nor subtract it) by appeal to the senses nor clear that any of the theorems of mathematics can be constructed without moving conceptually beyond what is given by their supposed elements or foundations. Further it is not clear that propositions as to God's existence are *not* verifiable, unless strictly sensuous verification is meant, of the sort that fails in every other sort of case as well. Nor is it established that a question must be answerable by some means in order that it be intelligible for it to be asked. We return, therefore, to the question of the existence of God.

By the very concept of God, as it emerges from the crucible of philosophical dialectic, it seems that a being of absolute perfection cannot fail to exist. Although the suggestion that the Absolute is that which cannot fail to be has been variously grasped or grasped at intuitively for many centuries, David Hume demonstrated quite conclusively that no existence can be established wholly *a priori*. In view of the preceding analysis, it seems very doubtful whether any proof of anything can be regarded as being wholly *a priori,* unless we could assume a proposition capable of proving itself or could regard a self-evident proposition as having been proved. Hume's argument, however, is somewhat more narrow. It urges, in effect, that no existential proposition can be demonstrated formally. For by formal or mathematical demonstration we can only elucidate (or I might say elaborate) what we have already assumed. The proposition 'God exists' plainly contains an existential operator, affirmatively applied to a certain alleged being (*i.e.,* one of infinite perfection). Unless that operator were contained in some premise of the argument from which this conclusion is to be derived and not only so contained but identically applied (either actually or potentially, say in virtue of its application to some class that includes God), it could never appear and be so applied in the conclusion. Thus if 'God exists' is to be deductively arrived at, it can only be by circularity. Which is to say, the celebrated ontological argument for the existence of God is based on the fallacy of *petitio principii*. But that assumes the object of that argument was to determine whether or not God exists.

What Hume demonstrates is that if we do not know that God exists no ontological argument—that is no argument from the concept of God we have—can demonstrate it. It does not demonstrate that the argument is invalid in the sense of involving an inconsistency. On the contrary, if we know that God exists or if we have some concept of God in which the idea of God's existence is implied, then positing that concept will imply God's existence as easily as may occur with regard to any other truism. For as surely as no deductive argument can yield conclusions stronger than its premises, no deductive argument should be required to yield conclusions less strong.

It may seem a strange procedure to argue God's existence from premises which contain already the assumption of that existence, but if the object in such a case is not to show that God exists when the existence of God was previously unknown then no *petitio* can be found in the procedure. In fact it is my confirmed suspicion that in the two most celebrated instances of formulations of the ontological argument something along the lines of such a procedure was at least in part just what was intended.

Anselm tells us that he wrote his ontological argument with an intention of reflecting in the self-containedness of his argument the self-sufficiency of his God.[7] And in responding to the monk who addressed him in behalf of the fool who said there is no God, Anselm called upon his religious brother in the name of what he hoped was a shared spritual experience by which he hoped an insight into the concept of God had been opened up—allowing the premise of his argument, God's perfection, to be made clear.[8] In other words, Anselm did not rest his argument before one who had no prior notion of divine existence. Similarly with Descartes.

It must puzzle any serious reader of the *Meditations* why Descartes offers to prove the existence of God twice. His first argument, in the Third Meditation is cosmological and thus *a posteriori*. The idea of perfection in his mind is treated as the effect of some cause which must be adequate ontically to the effect subjectively. Thus the cause of the idea of perfection must be Perfection itself. In the context of as yet unrelieved methodical doubt, the whole thought, although expressed as an argument based on causal reasoning on ontic premises regarding the precedence of perfection to privation and of actuality to ideality, must be construed as a single intuition, containing no parts, lest there be room here too for some deception. The intuition, then is that of the idea of perfection, conceived not in abstraction as a mere mathematical notion but rather as an expression of the Highest Perfection—an appeal to a conceptualized spiritual experience, if you will, but still an *a posteriori* argument. Why then the second proof of God's existence in the Fifth Meditation?

The object, I suspect, was not to establish God's existence for a second time, as the text seems to suggest,[9] but to establish the necessity of that existence, a conception which, as Spinoza remarked in analyzing the argument in question [10] was of the highest moment. For from the concept of necessary existence, as Maimonides had taught, it was possible to establish further the unity and absolute simplicity of God, the divine uniqueness, the ineffability of God, the inapplicability of all human notions and all attributes—in other words, the entire repertoire of natural theology, which is, as we have seen, a tradition of negative or transcendental theology.[11] All that could be said— or could not be said— of God followed from the conception of a necessary Being, and the latter concept followed from that of a Being of absolute perfection—thus the appropriateness of the ontological argument in its context in the *Meditations* of Descartes. It is not relied upon to prove the existence of God, which it rather takes for granted here, but it does establish all that Descartes believes can be established via natural theology as to the nature of God, divine existence having already been established, if the intuitive approach of the Third Meditation is regarded as acceptable and its verbal reliance on processes of causal inference and reasoning from presumptions as to ontological precedence are not regarded as vitiating its intuitive unity.

Thus in neither Anselm nor Descartes, as I view the matter, do we have an ontological demonstration of divine existence whose intended function is to show that God exists to those who do not accept that proposition. Rather we have two investigations of the concept of God, both aiming at revealing the elusive notion of necessary existence and neither founded on the notion that divine existence is in any way in doubt. The fallacy of which proponents of an ontological argument would be accused by Hume, then, does not apply in the case of Anselm or Descartes—at least to the extent that they did not imagine their arguments capable of demonstrating the existence of God outside a context where assertions of that existence were regarded as accepted. By the same token they did not in our familiar acceptation prove ontologically that God exists.

But even if the object of the ontological argument is not to prove that God exists, the notion of a necessary Being remains problematic, and it was here that Kant directed his attack. For Kant understood the aims of natural theology quite well. The concept of a necessary being, he argued, is incoherent, and any argument which relies upon that concept or invokes it in any way is fallacious. This, if true, would ruin all natural theology, for there is no coherent concept of God other than that of a being of absolute perfection, and that implies necessity of existence. Kant well knew that this is so. He is one philosophical critic of theology who fully recognized the intention of his opponents, and his undermining of natural theology is all the subtler and more sophisticated than that of Hume or Bayle for that reason. For it is not a simple or a feigned reversion through skepticism to unwitting faith that he professes. (For the ambiguity of that approach is not exhausted to this day. We all know that simple faith is not the sole response to doubts which reason cannot quell—and no one knows to this day for sure just where Hume stood, or Bayle, on the spectrum they projected between doubt and belief.) But Kant's was a very scriptural and very Christian reversion to morality as the sole basis of theology once the concept of a necessary Being had been undermined. Christian, because Christianity always feared the God of Abraham was too high to reach or to be reached by man and scriptural because morality was, along with cosmic wonder, authentically the foundation of Biblical theology—and prior to cosmic wonder in point of certitude and in point of integrative potential, if we have read our scriptural passages rightly. So Kant knew where to aim his guns. But was he right in supposing that the concept of a necessary Being is incoherent?

J. N. Findlay, who reached much the same conclusion as Kant in this regard once presented what he called an ontological *disproof* of the existence of God. By God, he writes, is meant a being which cannot not exist. But all existential propositions are synthetic, all are contingent; therefore, none are necessary. There can be, then, no necessary Being.

Only analytic propositions can be necessary, it is assumed, and these can never assert existence. The argument is founded upon Hume's dichotomy of matters of fact and relations of ideas. The latter can be dealt with only hypothetico-deductively and, therefore, can involve no facts, no categorical assertions of reality. The former, which we judge upon the foundations of experience, are not given as parts of some deductive system and can, therefore, involve no certainty of the mathematical sort—and certainly no necessity. To speak of God as a necessary Being, then, is to invoke some hybrid kind whose reality is less than problematic. Since experience is always contingent (it being always possible logically to postulate that things might have been other than as they are) so too must be existence. But to say that God is a necessary being, then, is tantamount to saying that God is both necessary and non-necessary, a *faux pas* only somewhat worse than saying He is and so must be regarded as a square circle.

But how do we know that being is entirely contingent? Does experience prove this to be so? We know that experience is variable. But experience does not give us all of being—unless we arbitrarily invoke the metaphysical equation of reality with seeming, and, at that, not merely with seeming to anyone, for of what may seem to anyone we have no notion, but only of what seems to ourselves. That is only if we adopt solipsism can we be assured that the contingency we discover in experience is a constant feature of reality. And even then we can have no assurance of that contingency's necessity nor any grounds to presume upon its persistence. That things might conceivably have been other than as they are does not prove that it is inevitable for all things to be contingent. The possibility of science (and indeed of any ordered system such as those of nature or of life) is predicated on the limitation of contingency, and the heuristic method of science is founded on the fiction (whether true or false is of no matter to the investigator) that in nature there is no contingency at all.

Findlay's criticism of the concept of a necessary Being is predicated on an analysis of the concept of necessity and on another of that of being. But we do not know that the only kind of necessity is logical necessity. Nor can we suppose, as we have seen, that logical necessity is absolute or absolutely to be distinguished from other sorts. We do not know that judgments can be so neatly classified objectively into analytic/formal and synthetic/material, for all judgments are synthetic, and any proposition may be treated as necessary or contingent depending on the context of presuppositions with which it is accompanied or from which it is abstracted. Findlay's argument presupposes that there is some necessity intrinsic in the relations of propositions and that this, which he calls logical necessity, is the only possible sort of necessity. But even this logical necessity requires reference beyond the necessary propositions to the system by which they are implied. And, even then, if all necessity is logical in this sense, then all is hypothetical, none categorical. Which means, in that case, there is no necessity at all.

The analysis of being which Findlay's ontological disproof presupposes is simply the extension of the Humean concept of necessity. For necessity, it is here assumed, is possible only with propositions which are logically related (by implication or exclusion) to others which have been posited. But with "matters of fact," considered as such, no such relations have been posited, so it is assumed that no type of necessity can be found. The proof is that no assumption bars the postulation of a hypothetical state of affairs quite different from that which actually obtains. And so it is assumed that all being is contingent. But if it is conceivable that some state of affairs is necessary in itself or rendered necessary by some cause quite apart from any formal necessitation of propositions by other propositions then it is impossible to say conclusively that all being is contingent, and the possibility of verbally denying any existential proposition without apparent contradiction proves nothing. Specifically it does not prove that realities which may be necessary are not so simply because there is no premised postulate which their denial would contradict. We simply do not know from the mere recognition of the formal possibility of denying any proposition whether all being is contingent or all necessary or some is necessary and some contingent or some perhaps is to be regarded as necessary in some respects and contingent in others.

The crux of Findlay's argument is that all being is contingent and, therefore, God, a non-contingent being, cannot exist. But the major premise is unknown and unknowable, highly problematic and quite possibly untrue.[12]

One of the crucial issues in the history of Western philosophy is the question whether existence is a characteristic (accident, properly expressible by a predicate) which things can either have or lack. When Aristotle exposed the fallacy of Parmenides' argumentation in behalf of monism, he made it very clear that in his belief the source of Parmenides' error lay in a failure to distinguish the existential from the copulative senses of the verb to be. According to Aristotle's analysis, as presented in the *Categories* and the *Metaphysics,* there is in fact no purely existential sense of the verb to be. 'Being' signifies in all the categories, and this systematic ambiguity is represented as exhausting the senses in which being is ascribed. Thus a subject either 'is ϕ' (where ϕ is a quality), or it is ψ (where ψ is a quanitity), or it is $\varkappa$ (where '$\varkappa$' names its species), and so forth through the ten categories. No subject can be designated unequivocally except under just one of the categories. Thus Aristotle argues that being itself is not a category or predicate but a systematically ambiguous cross categorical. To put the matter in medieval scholastic terminology, according to Aristotle being is not an accident, that is it is not a characteristic which a given thing can either have or lack. Thus, for example, Aristotle argued that things cannot be to different degrees, as would be the case if being were a quality. A thing either is or is not, by which Aristotle understood: it either is or is not ϕ, ψ, $\varkappa$, etc. Under the category of substance, which comes the closest to what we might call expressing existence, a thing either is or is not a man, a dog, etc. There is no way, according to Aristotle, by which a thing could be more or less a man say, or a dog.

The Platonic notion of participation, however, did seem to allow that things could be what they were to different degrees—for forms, at least, were ϕ (where ϕ expresses what the medievals called a perfection) to a higher degree than did the particulars which instantiated those forms. Thus being could be conceived as a property which any given subject might either have or lack. This notion of 'being' as a predicate made possible the Platonic conception that being is imparted to particulars from the forms. And Aristotle himself was not immune to this idea when he spoke in general terms[13] of things' deriving their actuality from that which was wholly actual—although he was always careful to make clear that he meant their actuality as ϕ, ψ, $\varkappa$, etc.

Even in antiquity Aristotle's doctrine of categories was not universally accepted. Both the Stoics and the neo-Platonists argued vigorously on a number of logical and linguistic grounds that existence is a category. Should there be no common theme running through the diverse uses of the verb to be, then all philosophers who had endeavored to salvage something of sense out of the heritage of Parmenidean monism, whether as the neo-Platonists did by finding formal unity in material diversity, or as the Stoics did by seeking organicity in physical nature, were destined to failure, and a pluralism of disparate and irreducible principles would inevitably triumph, a pluralism which the Aristotelians themselves could hardly welcome since it would defeat their efforts at the integration of experience. Moreover, if being was not a property, then being could not be something imparted to particulars by God and could not form a natural/ontic scale in terms of which human beings could seek their perfection—as both the Stoics and the neo-Platonists in their different ways believed it did.

The rise of Jewish, Christian, and Islamic monotheism gave further dimension to the import of the doctrine that being is a predicate. For one of the prime functions of myth[14] is the imparting of insight, the capability of appreciating the way things are, and one of the prime methods by which myth achieves this aim is by an elementary fictive abstraction which demands that one regard things from the perspective of the assumption that they need not have been as they are but might have been otherwise. The book of *Genesis* achieves this aim in a con-summate way by forcing its audience to imagine the entire world as once having not existed and thus demanding consideration of the sort of conditions which could have given it being. Thus the book of *Genesis* requires its audience to look upon being as a characteristic which things might or might not have had.

The Muslim philosopher Abû 'Alî Ibn Sînâ (Avicenna, 980–1037) transformed this sort of insight into a philosophic argument. Being, he argued, is an accident. For with any conceivable finite thing one may always imagine that it does or that it does not exist. In "modern" philosophic discourse, the same fact is often expressed by the familiar dictum that all existential propositions are synthetic. By this is meant that the notion of existence is a distinct one from our conception of the essence of the subject under discussion, for it is said that this notion of existence must be added (by way of predication) to that of the subject when existence is ascribed to anything we conceive. This is exactly what Avicenna meant by calling existence an accident.[15] As a rationalist Avicenna believed that all facts require an explanation and thus that all contingent facts (*i.e.,* all which might have been otherwise than as they are) must be explained in terms of factors extrinsic to themselves (*i.e.,* factors not comprised in the notion of the contingent facts in question). For if a fact could be understood solely in terms of itself then it would not be contingent but necessary. In the case of any contingent fact, then, Avicenna believed that one is led inevitably to a system and sequence of causes, and this consideration was the basis of his version of an argument for the existence of God, which I would call an argument *ex contingentia* or contingency argument, but which Kant called the Cosmological Proof.

The argument, which Kant says "is too well known to require detailed statement," is simply this:

1. Something exists.

For I exist, this sense object exists (the ancients were generally realists)— even if it is claimed that all is illusion, that illusion exists.

2. What does exist (as conceded in 1) is either necessary or contingent.

That is it either contains or does not contain within itself the conditions of its own determinate existence. This is a necessary disjunction. But if it does contain those conditions it is a necessary being. If it does not, it must have a cause for its (determinate) existence, *i.e.,* for its being at all and its being as and how it is. This cause too is either necessary or contingent. But (Avicenna argued) there cannot be an infinite sequence of causes or they would never reach the actual effect, which, *ex hypothesi* (by 1), they have. For the early links in such a chain, it is argued, would not have been real and had their determinate effects had not the links prior to them already been made actual by actually existing causes, so there must have been an actual first cause, *i.e.,* an ultimate link in the sequence, from which the causal action stems. Or so it was assumed. Thus the causal sequence has an origin, and at its origin there is a being which contains the conditions of its own existence within itself, *i.e.,* a necessary being. But a necessary being cannot not exist and therefore must be simple (ungenerated, indestructible), changeless, eternal, and absolutely perfect (pure actuality), in other words, it must be divine. The core of the argument is that the assumption of a contingent being logically requires the assumption of a necessary (and therefore divine) being.[16]

Kant bases his critique of the cosmological argument upon his refutation of the ontological argument, for both, he says, are based upon the spurious notion of a necessary being. Kant's critique of the ontological argument is based upon two lines of argument, closely linked in his presentation, one of which assumes that 'being' is a predicate and the other of which assumes that it is not.

The first of Kant's two arguments runs as follows: The notion of an ontological argument is centered upon that of a necessary being. But this must be rephrased in terms of the lessons of post-Humean critical philosophy. It is not beings but propositions which may be necessary. If there is a necessary being, that could only mean a being whose existence it is self-contradictory to deny, *i.e.,* a being for whom the notion of existence was comprised in *its* notion so that one could not consider it coherently without granting its existence. This would be a case not merely of a predicate being required by its subject but of a subject which could not coherently not be posited. That after all is what is claimed by the ontological argument. But that, Kant argues is impossible. For "every reasonable person" must admit "that all existential propositions are synthetic."[17] For if such propositions could be analytic, the assertion of the existence of a necessary being would be "a miserable tautology."[18]

More tellingly, we know that all existential propositions are synthetic because it is never self-contradictory to deny such propositions. If we are to interpret this last claim in any way that avoids making Kant's refutation of the ontological argument circular, then we must assume that it applies only to assertions of the existence of finite beings. For if the assertion of the existence of an infinite being is included without warrant being given for that assertion, then the question has been begged.

With regard to the existence of finite beings, of course, the claim is true. There may be, to be sure, a formal contradiction in the assertion of the existence of a certain being and the simultaneous assertion of the existence of another whose reality is *by postulate* understood to be incompatible with that of the first. If so there can be, correspondingly, a logical necessity implying the reality of a being whose existence is *by postulate* necessitated by that of another whose reality is postulated. But in the simple assertion of a given finite being's reality, without reference to any other state of affairs there can be no contradiction of any kind— unless it is the contradiction of some tacit assumption imported into the terms of that assertion which renders it in effect a compound proposition, one element of which is contradictory to another. And by the same token there can be no self-contradiction in the denial of the existence of any finite thing.

With any finite real thing, conditions invariably may be conceived which would curtail the existence of that thing—for, by definition, it is a thing whose existence is curtailed, and that by other things. So, of no finite thing can it be said that its essence necessitates that it exist. But the same reasoning cannot be applied to an infinite thing—no more than can an analogy with our experience with finite things, which seem to originate and to cease existing in fact. An infinite being, by definition, cannot be curtailed in its existence. The prevention of its existence cannot be required by something else, and it is difficult to see how its existence can be prevented by itself.

The plausibility of Kant's claim that there is never a contradiction in the denial of any existence is founded on the intellectual abstraction by which he isolates each particular assertion of existence in question from any considerations regarding its conditions, the supporting or curtailing factors surrounding the being whose existence is affirmed. But the credibility of such conditioning is confined to the realm of finite objects. What Kant must show if his argument is to have force is that there is no self-contradiction in denying the reality of an infinite being. This seems questionable on the face of it, and it seems doubtful, if the notion is to be entertained, how it would be known. Clearly it cannot be inferred from our experience (or linguistic policies?) regarding the denial of the reality of finite things. Thus Kant cannot establish in this way the inappropriateness of the notion of necessary existence.

More importantly for the present investigation, the truth of the assertion that all existential propositions (regarding any finite, determinate entity) are synthetic depends upon the recognition that (for such entities at least) essence is distinguishable from existence, that is upon the admission that the question what a thing is is a different question from the question whether it exists. And that, precisely, is what Avicenna meant when he claimed that existence (meaning finite existence) is an accident, *i.e.*, a property which any entity may either have or lack; in modern language, 'being' is a predicate. That Avicennan assumption of the (logical) contingency of all (finite) being is the basis of Kant's claim that all existential propositions are synthetic.

Kant's second argument is founded on the contradictory of the underlying assumption of his first. The illusion which lends an air of plausibility to the ontological fallacy, he claims is the confusion of a logical with a real predicate. " 'Being,' " he writes, "is obviously not a real predicate; that is, it is not a concept of something which could be added to the concept of a thing. It is merely the positing of a thing, or of certain determinations, as existing in themselves. Logically it is merely the copula of judgment."[19] The notion of existence in no way adds to the determinations of a thing. There is no difference whatever in conception between a hundred real thalers and a hundred possible or imaginary thalers.[20]

When Kant says that being is not a separate or separable notion from the determinations of things he is directly contradicting Avicenna's claim that existence (in finite things) is an accident, *i.e.*, a notion distinct from and not implied by the notion of the things themselves. If existence were an added or determining notion, Kant argues, then the thing whose existence I assert would not be the same as the thing whose existence I deny or merely consider. This argument, it must be pointed out, rests on a verbal fallacy, for when we consider the existence or non-existence of any given thing we are performing an act of abstraction. In a very definite sense it is *not* the same thing which is regarded as existing that is regarded as not existing. This exactly parallels the case with what are universally confessed to be predicates: In a very definite sense it is not the same dog I speak of when I ask you to assume by an act of mental abstraction that my dog might have been a different color or sex than it is. Here the predicate is admitted to make a difference. But existence is abstracted in just the same way, and in the same way it can be said that in a sense it is not the same thing which exists and which is considered as possibly existing—*i.e.*, that existence too makes a difference.

Kant's claim is that the notion of existence serves only to posit a given set of determinations. Such positing is, of course, entirely a function of judgment, and some such positing is a necessary condition of the entertaining of any sort of thought on a given subject. One is tempted to ask what distinguishes the hypothetical positing of a given imaginary or possible subject from the positing of a real one—or what distinguishes the positing of a subject thought to be real from that of a subject assumed not to be real—for this is the crucial element designated by the assertion (in earnest) of existence. And, as Kant himself points out, it makes a very real difference to his finances whether there is a real or imaginary hundred thalers in his pocket. Kant's argument is that if there were any real difference between the possible being posited in one judgment and the actual being posited in another then it would be impossible to say that the judgment made about an actual being as actual deals with the same entity as a related judgment as to a possible being, considered as possible. But in a very real sense the two judgments do not deal with the same being, for the transition from one to the other involves the abstraction of a by no means unimportant element in the concept assumed—that of existence. The very possibility of speaking of the "same" subject now as existing, now as not existing rests upon the underlying assumption Avicenna would have expressed by saying that existence is "a super-added notion" not given in the essence of a thing considered by itself. Which is to say existence is an accident, or in modern terms, a predicate. So now, in contrast to his earlier claim, Kant rests his argument on the assertion that 'existence' is *not* a predicate, *i.e.,* that reality is not an accident or determination of a thing, a notion added to that of the thing's essence or distinct from it. And this premise is directly contradictory to the premise of his first argument, that all existential propositions are synthetic. For the only meaning which the former premise can have is that existence *is* a notion distinct from that of the essence of a thing and to that extent does determine it.

The natural defense for those who would wish to rescue Kant from this embarrassing situation would be to choose for him one of his two arguments and reject the other. (There are, as I have shown, good grounds for the rejection of either, for the the plausibility of the first rests on the syntheticity of existential judgments regarding *finite* beings, and the second seems to gain credence by a purely semantic fiat which declares existence not to be a determination, hence not to be a predicate—despite the very real difference which existence can make with regard to almost any subject.) But if forced to choose between Kant's first and second refutations of the ontological argument, the Kantian will be rather hard put to it. For the question whether existence actually is or is not a predicate, *i.e.,* a real determination, despite Kant's conflicting assertions that " 'Being' is obviously not a real predicate" and (on the same page) that every reasonable person must admit that all existential propositions are synthetic, is precisely the sort of question which critical philosophy is supposed to render unaskable, and the conflicting approaches Kant develops to its answer might well be added to the list of the antinomies of pure reason, were it not fairly clear that they are simply corollaries of the antithetical views of the first antinomy. For the doctrine that all existential propositions are synthetic is based, as we have seen, on the assumption of the contingency of being (symbolized by the Biblical idea of the createdness of the world), while the doctrine that 'existence' is not a predicate is intimately bound up, as Kant's own argument makes clear, with the Aristotelian claim that being cannot be abstracted (*i.e.,* with the eternity of the world). For this claim is based upon the alleged inseparability of existence from the concept of any thing—or, at least, we must insist, of any *real* thing; for the antinomy here arises from considering possible beings in the one instance, real beings thought of as such, in the other, a confusion identical to that by which Kant himself explains the antinomy between creation and eternity.

Kant fails to recognize that in attempting to settle once for all the most metaphysical question of the validity or invalidity of the ontological argument he has fallen into the trap of a typical antinomy of pure reason without having provided himself with any metaphysical base by which to escape. As soon as he broaches the question it becomes almost inevitable that he will put himself in the position of saying that all existential propositions are synthetic, *i.e.,* that the predicate adds something not contained in the subject, and then continuing, almost as though he were arguing from the same premises, "By whatever and by however many predicates we may think a thing—even if we completely determine it—we do not make the least addition to the thing when we further declare that this thing *is.*"[21] I say that such an outcome as this became inevitable or virtually inevitable as soon as Kant had broached the subject of the ontological argument because in attempting to determine whether or not existence is a predicate Kant has violated his own principle that the limits of pure reason do not extend to the resolution of such issues, and it was only natural, given the many conflicting claims one encounters as to the logic of 'being' that he should invoke one which considers things from the point of view of their possibility and another which looks at them from the point of view of assuming their actuality.

Whether one regards the ontological argument as in fact fallacious depends to a great extent on what one understands by 'God.' Thus in Spinoza's thought, for example, the proof that there is a necessary being is entirely unproblematic. For, if anything exists, something must exist self-sufficiently. And, given that all things are determined both as to their existence and as to the conditions of their existence, this implies that something exists necessarily.[22] Or if God is understood to be the totality of all that is, it seems inevitable that God exists, provided that anything exists at all. A more adventuresome proposition in Spinoza is that what is real must be infinite perfection expressed in infinite ways; and thus, in Spinoza's sense, divine.[23] To the Greeks it did not seem at all self-evident that a necessary being must be either infinite or divine. The atoms of Democritus and of Epicurus, for example, were necessary beings, for they were uncaused; being themselves primal causes, they were un- conditioned; and, being indestructible, they could be said to have no conditions under which they did not exist. It might be objected that it is not self-contradictory to deny the existence of a Democritean or Epicurean atom, and that is true; but even that claim must be qualified, for to deny absolute solidity (the atom) according to Epicurus is to contradict sense experience, which in *his* canonic is tantamount to self- contradiction; and it is clear that Democritus regarded *his* atoms as possessed of that inalienable existence which Parmenides had claimed for the primal unity: The Democritean atom was equated with being (the void, non-being), which it was self-contradictory to deny.

The appeal to Parmenidean logic in behalf of the necessity of being as applied to finite things is still more evident in the case of Aristotle. For, given the doctrine of the categories, that a thing cannot be said simply to be but must be said to be either 'a this' or 'a that,' Aristotle was fully prepared to accept what he took to be the truth of the assertion of Parmenides that what is must be, by which he understood that the species of all things which exist must exist and have the natures that they have and that there would be a self-contradiction in the claim that they need not exist or have those natures.

In this sense we can see that the ontological argument is not an issue in Aristotle's philosophy, not because he had no concept of necessary being, but because he regarded all realities (the species of things and the cosmos with its "principal parts," the heavens) as necessary beings whose existence one could not coherently deny.[24] Their essences com- prised their existence for him; indeed, as his analysis of 'being' in the *Metaphysics* shows, their existence (being) was their essence (their being what they were).[25] It was Avicenna, rendering an old insight philosophically explicit, under the influence of the Islamic *Kalâm,* ultimately under the influence of the powerful Hebraic dichotomy between necessary and contingent being, who confined the notion of ontic necessity to God and argued not only for the reality of a necessary being as a precondition of contingent being but also for the tran- scendence of all finite categories by the necessary being which contingent reality requires if we are not to regard its contingency as self-sufficing.

But it was Anselm, not Avicenna, who tried to make the notion of

God's self-sufficiency and absolute perfection the proof of God's existence—albeit not, perhaps to a "fool" or unbeliever. The intuition of some such argument as this had been implicit in the thinking of Plato and of Parmenides before him—the notion that a being of absolute perfection, pure actuality, or however it was later to be expressed, could not fail to exist. But Anselm perhaps came the closest to expressing the idea in an argument. What is wrong with Anselm's argument, I think, at least if it is hoped that it may be put to use in some controversial context as a weapon with which to combat unbelief, is best gotten at by Aquinas' distinction between analyticity and self-evidence. Aquinas grants that God is an absolutely perfect being, and from this it follows, he concedes, that God exists. But not everyone, Aquinas points out, need share this highly sophisticated conception of divinity, which, as Aquinas learned from Maimonides, may involve lengthy argumentation to establish[26] or perhaps special intuitions of a revelatory nature. Indeed it may be argued that the fulness of God's perfection is known only to Him. And thus it might indeed be said that while the ontological argument may be valid its validity is comprehended fully only by God. Anselm himself intimates his awareness that this might be how the issue lies when he appeals to Gaunilon's religious faith and experience. The concept of God which the ontological argument unfolds is one which might be derived from extended analysis of the logic of God or perhaps from faith or revelation, it is not one which would be held by a naif or a fool. The "fool" of the psalm (actually one who acts on the assumption that there is no accountability before God for human actions) is taken in the philosophic glosses to be one who has not yet surpassed a stage which views the existence of God as problematic. From such a standpoint, naturally, the ontological argument would be a plain case of question begging.

But given the concept of God as absolute perfection and given the possibility of treating being as "an accident" or, as Descartes more pointedly puts it, as a perfection, it is clear that there is no simple fallacy in the ontological argument such as Kant claimed. If being is a perfection and God's perfection is absolute, then the being which God has must be necessary, and the necessity of that being will be obscure only to one who persists in conceiving God in categories appropriate only to finite or imperfect, contingent beings. Kant fails to expose a formal fallacy in the ontological argument but succeeds only in showing that that argument is not a suitable way of "proving" the existence of God to one who so utterly misconceives the idea of God as to regard the divine existence in itself as problematic. But since Kant's refutation of the cosmological argument depends on his refutation of the ontological and specifically on his alleged demonstration of the incoherence of the concept of a necessary being, that too fails. If there is no contradiction implicit in the concept of necessary existence, then there can be no flaw in the cosmological argument derived solely from its use of the idea of a necessary being. Nevertheless, Kant has more cogent arguments to direct against the contingency argument than he has against the ontological argument. For the classic contingency argument, as we have seen, assumes the impossibility of an infinite causal regress, and that assumption may be called into question from a conflicting point of view. It may be possible, however, to distill more fully what is being gotten at in the contingency argument by eliminating that premise and reducing the argument to this:

There must be a reason for things' being as they are, either within them or beyond them, but finite things cannot contain the totality of the determinants by which they are conditioned, hence there must be an infinite and transcendent cause of those determinations (including the determination of being over non-being).

All rationalist theists have seen clearly that the matter must be stated in such a way as this if it is to be stated at all, and Leibniz made explicit the assumption which all had made at least implicitly: that if the reason for things' being as they are is not within them then (as Spinoza put it) it must be extrinsic to them. The assumption is that if things have a determinate nature or character (including the character of existing rather than not existing), then something has determined that character. To some rationalists, such as Averroes this implication appeared to be a tautology. If things were not determined, Averroes argued, then they must be undetermined. It would follow trivially that they must have remained indeterminate—which implication contradicts our actual experience, and for that matter, all possible or at least conceivable modes of actual experience. Leibniz was undoubtedly more sophisticated, recognizing that the principle of sufficient reason was not a law of logic but a metaphysical assumption. Nevertheless it seemed somehow an assumption one was obliged to make.

It was Hume who taught Kant the alternative: That things need not be as they are. Where Avicenna, as a rationalist, had argued that since there is no contradiction in assuming that what is not is, there must therefore be a transcendent cause (*i.e.,* one beyond the natures of the things) to make things as they are, Hume reversed the field, arguing that since there is no contradiction in things' being other than as they are there is *no* transcendental reason (*i.e.,* none beyond the nature of the mind) why they need be as they are. The price of choosing this alternative, however, is the abandonment of the rationalist program and conception of ex-planation, or at the very least the confinement of the program within the boundaries of a specific conceptual game. In either case we lose the ability to explain.

The notion of explanation is a rationalist and a realist concept and is to be explicated, in my view, in rationalist-realist terms. To explain is in the broadest sense to answer or resolve a question, that is to alleviate a doubt. This involves a requirement that the data we possess must be deducible from any explanation which is to account for them. I can explain the drops of water on my car seat by the assumption that it has rained while I was in the store, that the window was left open and the wind blowing in a particular direction. Given a sufficient set of such assumptions the appearances I observe will follow as a matter of deductive implication, although, of course there are an infinitude of alternative sets of explanatory assumptions from which the same data could be derived.

Explanation differs from other forms of question answering in that it does not merely fill the gap left by a question but fills in the area around and behind that gap, not only relieving a doubt but affording an ability to answer other, related questions and to recognize the basis of the relationships among related questions. Thus it affords a bigger satisfaction than an answer to a single question, satisfying a more general curiosity than that aroused by a single isolated query. Explanation is necessarily metaphysical in that it involves assumptions about the nature of the world.

Explanation as I understand it, moreover, involves the uncovering of a correspondence between the notions we develop of things in our empirical experience of them and other notions which we find to be somehow satisfactory on grounds of aesthetic or logical completeness, symmetry, or some such formal characteristic or on grounds of relatedness (analogy) to some comparable pattern regarding matters which are assumed to be understood. The discovery of such a correspondence is understanding. Its revelation or explication is explanation.

It may be thought that the formal or material categories against which experience is measured are fabrications of the mind imposed upon phenomena to create an arbitrary order. But if that is so there is no explanation. In explanation the order posited by the mind is regarded as objective and external. That is the realism inherent in the notion of explanation. One is not said to explain things' being as they are simply by an ordering of phenomena in an arbitrary categoreal framework but only when what is regarded as the actual arrangement of things has been confronted with an explanatory paradigm or pattern. This pattern may be thought to be made up *ad hoc* out of the strictly empirical materials of experience. But, if this is so, once again we have no explanation. The categories of the paradigm must be at least in part *a priori,* otherwise there is no discovery involved in the ascertainment of correspondence or fit. Thus even in analogy, which might seem, perhaps, to be wholly *a posteriori* since it involves the comparison of one discovered pattern with another, there is resort (as Plato noted long ago when he refuted radical empiricism) to the *a priori* category of likeness. And again, all causal explanations involve an element of the *a priori* in that they involve such concepts as material necessitation, universal uniformity, transcendental reality—none of which is encountered as an empirical phenomenon.

One does not explain the behavior of a planet simply by presenting a table of its sightings. (At least that is not what is meant by explanation outside the sphere of influence of a certain viewpoint regarding formal epistemology). But one comes closer when one recognizes a uniform pattern, as of a circle (element in an incorrect explanation) or ellipse (element in a corrected explanation) in those data, closer still when that path has been described according to a rule, and even closer when the forces governing the adherence of phenomena to that path have been enumerated, related to one another and to as many other variables as can be so related and the mathematics of their relationship worked out. I do not know if there can ever be a comprehensive explanation of any one phenomenon or whether that is (as I suspect) an ideal which finite but increasing understanding may approach but must always continue to view from a distance. I do know that in empiric terms no explanation is ever absolutely conclusive, as an infinitude of alternative explanations are always available to account for a given set of phenomena.[27]

It is in the correspondence of an objective pattern with a somehow mentally satisfying and in part *a priori* pattern that explanation consists, and it is in this satisfaction of having found or heard a more or less adequate explanation that the satisfaction of explanations lies. There are other notions of explanation than the one which I have offered here, but none involve an accounting for the peculiar efficacy which is characteristic of explanation in its most familiar sense. For if explanation is simply the marshalling of data there is no satisfying "fit." A pattern which recommends itself to the mind is required for that. This involves not only the ability to deduce the data from the explanation, but also values such as economy and elegance, symmetry perhaps, or some other logical, mathematical or aesthetic properties such as completeness or continuity. Again, if the mental or ideal patterns applied are regarded as just that and not thought to represent objective realities, then again there is no fit, for the data in such a case is now thought of as in actuality amorphous or unknown, the "explanation" as a pure fiction and hence of no explanatory power.

Rationalism in its moderate form is the belief that some things are intelligible, that is that some aspects of objective reality answer to forms and categories of understanding. Rationalism in its strong form is the belief that all things are intelligible. Positivism, the alternative to rationalism, likewise has two forms, a moderate form which holds that some things are unintelligible, not explainable but simply are—that is as positive, irreducible or unrelatable facts. The strong form of positivism holds that all facts are irreducible, unintelligible, unrelatable objectively to broader patterns and unassimilable to significant categories but that the effort to discover pattern or intelligible significance in phenomena is idle play. This is the position of radical empiricism which regards phenomena not only as primary but as ultimate and sufficient. It is the position in law which rests content with the positive dictum of the statute without seeking intent, justification, purpose, goal or utility. And the same spirit manifests itself in many other branches of inquiry.

The moderate positions of rationalism and positivism are compatible with one another, since neither makes a universal claim. The unqualified variety of positivism is compatible with no form of rationalism, thus with no form of explanation. The unqualified variety of rationalism is compatible with no form of positivism.

But unqualified positivism is an incoherent doctrine. For it pronounces a general dictum on existence as a whole and thus is an attempt at comprehensive explanation—but the pattern it assigns (although quite satisfying in some ways aesthetically and logically in virtue of its totality and uniformity) is the absence of all pattern, the impossibility of all explanation or intelligibility. Unqualified positivism thus rests upon a paradox; or, as it might more pointedly be expressed, it rests on self-contradiction, inasmuch as it seeks to render reality at large intelligible through the general pronouncement that reality at large is unintelligible.[28]

The same may be observed of the moral (rather than epistemological) positivism which has arisen in the existentialist tradition. Here moral stands become isolated from all universal significance, and the sense that nature and the world do not answer to the categories of moral judgment creates that sense of forlornness known in the existential phenomenology as the death of God. Absurdity here is not the isolation of one fact from another and of all from a general pattern but rather the parallel isolation of the 'for-itself' from the 'in-itself,' of one subject from another and of all moral judgments from the universal justification which, implicitly, they claim. Meaninglessness here is not the impossibility of the mind's discovering a universal causal law alleged by the epistemological positivists, but the parallel impossibility alleged of human moral sense legislating a universal moral law. For the moral law, to be moral, must be free; yet, to be law, it must be universally imposed. It is from this alleged paradox, arising from a misconception of the manner in which a moral law is imposed (for it is not and cannot be externally imposed but must be freely chosen and internally appropriated, universally, and is none the less free for that), that the existentialist sense of (moral) absurdity arises, paralleling the epistemic sense that there is no universal causal law or principle with a more anguished sense that there is no higher moral law or principle.

But this position too, a variant or special case of radical positivism, is incoherent. For the powers from which its paradox draws its force are values, the value (or necessity) of freedom in moral choice juxtaposed with the value of fairness or universality in moral law. The paradox is vitiated if these values are not of objective significance. The absurdist conclusion, if taken as leading to the undermining of all objective moral judgments, is contradicted by its own premises.

In both the moral and the epistemic case, a radical positivism is not only incoherent but daily and each moment contradicted by the discourse of human experience. For we do explain and judge morally. It is by means of this fact that *Ecclesiastes* overcomes the sense of global insignificance mooted in the opening lines of the text. For the global assessment that all is empty, vain or meaningless presupposes some accepted standards of value. And while any of these alone might fail of totality and fall short of giving worth to life in isolation and abstraction from one another, taken together in due counterbalance with one another they may point toward a meaningful existence.[29] Similarly in epistemic terms, the very notion that something is inexplicable is predicated on the assumption that the notion of explaining has some sphere of legitimate application. Otherwise it would be unintelligible to use the term. Some eastern philosophers have imagined that logical categories may be employed merely dialectically, only to undermine all logical categories. Were such a method to be applicable in the present context, it would be necessary for explanation itself to be explained away, and that plainly is impossible. The denial of intelligibility, then, whether in moral or in epistemic terms presupposes that something is intelligible in such terms. Which is to say that if any positivism is coherent it can only be some variety which is not absolutely comprehensive.

It may seem that the extreme form of rationalism is as easily refuted as the extreme form of positivism and that therefore a hybrid of moderate rationalism and moderate positivism must be left holding the field. For it seems self-evident that not all things can be explained. If nature contains an infinitude of facts, then not all can be enumerated. But if what is to be explained is a finite body of data then some items must be explained in terms of others and some must remain unexplained in order that the rest may be treated without circularity, just as Euclid and the Dictionary are forced to leave some terms undefined if circularity is to be avoided.

But this reasoning is specious. For finite explanations may account for infinite data, as they do in all formulations of scientific laws which account for phenomena in the unobserved future as well as in the observable present. And the first principles of explanation need not be unexplained but may be self-explanatory, leaving no surds at all in the conceptual system. Here arises the quarrel between an unqualified rationalism, which regards all things as intelligible and that tempered or qualified rationalism which treats all things as intelligible *except* first principles, which are taken to be positive data, for which no explanation is conceivable.

Once again, however, I shall claim that a rationalism qualified by positivism is incoherent. For although it renders some things intelligible by reference to others, it presumes upon an understanding of those other things which ultimately it cannot provide. Logically speaking, this is a kiting operation, a drawing on resources borrowed on the strength of credit for which (at the final remove) there is no collateral, an effort to fly simply by running faster and faster in circles. In rationalism which ends in positivism nothing is explained in any ultimate way, for the first principles to which all explanations are held to be reducible are themselves left unintelligible. A qualified rationalism, in other words, is equivalent to pure positivism ultimately; although explanatory formats are used, they lead to data for which there is no explanation given or allowed for.

The alternative is to uncover some elements of explanation which are self-explanatory. The endeavor to discover some first principle or *arche* of all material things which was practiced by the Greek *physikoi* and survives in the continued search for an ultimate particle by some investigators into physics is, it seems, in part, a search for some explanatory principle which will require no further explanation—or one, indeed, for which no explanation is possible. This conception is very much in line with that of Democritus and other early atomists for whom the atom was pure being, which neither came to be nor passed away but simply was (and is, and will be) without cause or further element.

But is such atomism, taken as a paradigm of pure rationalism, purely rationalistic? Does it find a principle which is self-explanatory and presents the conditions of its own existence? Or does it merely present a principle which is unexplained and seek a principle which is unexplainable? In that case, what it represents is not pure rationalism at all but rationalism qualified (and, as we have seen, vitiated) by positivism. For the atom, the element, the world itself, does not explain itself. It does not establish the conditions of its own finite determination. Or, as Saadya put it, it does not (and, being limited, cannot) create itself. Leibniz was keenly alive to the dilemma of atomism. If the sought-for ultimate particle has size, it can be divided and so must be a composite, required to be explained in terms of *its* elements. If, on the other hand, it has no size? What then? This is the avenue taken by the occasionalistic *kalâm*. They identify dimensionless atoms as "being." If an atom has no size or other dimension of its own (*i.e.,* duration), then it is not the ultimate explanatory principle by which all phenomena are to be explained. For this atom is to explain things in virtue of its constituting them and thus should have or be capable of generating the properties they have. But the things made up by atoms have duration, relation, continuity, and these are extrinsic to "being," that is to the atom, if it is assumed to be dimensionless in accordance with that radical conception of the contingency of being upon which the *Mutakallimûn* predicated their understanding of the contrast between God and nature.

But radical contingency is not necessary for this contrast to be drawn. Any finitude in being as *we* understand it will suffice. We still can ask of any finite or determinate thing—of the atom, of the chemical elements, of the electron—why it shows the size and shape, the properties and behavior that it shows. And if those atoms or elements have been treated as ultimate principles of explanation, no answer can be forthcoming, for the ultimate cannot be explained by that which it has explained, nor can finite "ultimates" explain their own determinations. If they could, it would be impossible for them to have any other than they do. But such a possibility is far from inconceivable. Of course, it may be objected that this conceivability proves nothing, on the same grounds that I have pled earlier myself—that the impossibility of ultimate causes' being other than as they are may be intrinsic rather than logical. An ultimate principle of this sort, however, could not be causally conditioned, a rather suspicious property in some body to be located in nature. But the notion of intrinsic necessity still may not seem logically impossible for a natural object. The necessary body might have parts. The argument in this case is not that its divergence from its present state is inconceivable but only intrinsically impossible. Being finite it is not ˜divine. But being unchangeable or of set form, its putative role as a first cause in nature is at best highly problematic. A natural, physical cause of motion, as Aristotle argued long ago, would seem to need to be in motion itself. But the notion of a physical unmoved mover is not logically impossible in itself. What refutes the notion of a finite first principle is not any inconceivability in the notion but simply the extreme remoteness of the notion of the idea from our physics—the remoteness of the notion of a physical cause of change which is unchanged by change. Reasoning cannot ever eliminate totally the possibility that the ultimate principle of all things is finite. To attempt to do so would be to belie the empirical dimension of all explanation, the necessary inconclusiveness of all causal inferences, for which we have argued.

But the fact remains that even in the case that finite things are allowed to have an intrinsic necessity to be just as they are, we are left with an unexplained positivity. Rationalism remains incomplete. And so it must remain unless the ultimate principle of explanation is infinite, which is to say divine. This is the theistic option. It is not demonstrated by necessity of logic, for we are speaking here of matters of fact, in regard to which our best notions are and must be mere hypotheses. The monotheistic hypothesis is that the causal principle (which Leibniz labelled the principle of sufficient reason) that things which might have been otherwise require a cause to make them as they are (which is not a law of logic but a general rule of inquiry and of scientific method) should not be dropped arbitrarily when we reach the level of ultimates, but that rationalism should be pressed consistently, no residue of unresolved positivity retained. The outcome is that the ultimate explanatory principle must itself become explicable, not by analysis into parts or relation to causes ulterior to the ultimate but by reference to Itself. Which is to say, the ultimate causal/explanatory principle must be self-contained, perfect and absolute—infinite in other words, or divine.

It is possible to respond, of course, that there is no need that anything be explained and certainly no need for the explanation of ultimates. But this claim is specious, as I have endeavored to show. Explanation is a category from which there is no abstraction. Alternatively it may be claimed that finite first principles may be self-explanatory. This is not inconceivable, allowing that their required necessity is intrinsic and not logical. But no likely candidate appears for a self-explanatory finite first principle. Spinoza offered good grounds (which he may have thought were conclusive proof) why there can be none: What is finite not only conditions but is conditioned by other finite things. This need not be so by logic in the abstract, but empirically the grounds for believing that it *is* so in fact seem to remain as good as they were when Spinoza concluded other-conditionedness to be inevitable among finite things.

Monotheism is the belief, well-grounded in an understanding of nature, that the ultimate is absolute and for that reason not finite. This requires the seeking for a transcendent God. That result is not surprising. As Saadya argued, if it is the principle to which we refer all realities of nature that we seek, we should not expect to find that principle *within* nature, among the very actualities which we seek to explain.[30] On the contrary, it must transcend nature. It was this concept, I think, that the ultimate explanatory principle of the world must be absolute, infinite and perfect, transcending all reduction to the world's categories but explicable solely in itself, that was expressed in the words, "In the beginning God created heaven and earth."

---

1. *Cf. Exodus* 33:20: "Thou canst not see My face, for man shall not see me and live." God can cause His goodness to pass before Moses, but even the prophet is denied direct apperception of God. He can confront God conceptually, through the "pellucid lens" of a purified intellect, but not perceptually, or the very concept of absolute perfection would be negated. *Cf.* MAIMONIDES' *Eight chapters,* ch. 7.

John Hick, a contemporary philosopher, seems to construe 'man shall not see My face and live' as 'man shall not see My face *while living,*' arguing that when we have died we shall be afforded that direct perceptual (?!) proof of God's reality which is denied during life. (See "Theology and Verification," reprinted from *Theology Today* in John Hick, ed. *The Existence of God,* New York, 1964.) Christian faith, Hick argues, is verifiable, eschatologically. He illustrates with a parable of two men "traveling together along a road. One of them believes that it leads to a Celestial City, the other that it leads nowhere; but since this is the only road there is, both must travel it. . . They do not entertain different expectations about the coming details of the road, but only about its ultimate destination. And when they do turn the last corner it will be apparent that one of them has been right all the time and the other wrong. . . . Christian doctrine postulates an ultimate unambiguous state of existence *in patria* as well as our present ambiguous existence *in via..*" (Pp. 260–261)

But how can there be a last turning on a road that leads toward Infinity? Or how can a finite being while finite (thus conscious of itself as distinguished from the objects of its awareness—or as the Bible expresses it, alive) transcend doubt and be granted certainty? We must bear in mind that Hick addresses his notion of eschatological verification not to the question of religious doubt in general, although he does situate Christian claims within their larger context of 'hope' but also specifically to the question of the existence of God; and here the mythic approach has insurmountable drawbacks. For if we do in some future state (of which the Pentateuch knows nothing) confront some being which convinces us of a certainty (at least phenomenologically) that it is God or represents God, how do we know that we are right in embracing such a (seeming) certainty? Perhaps the apparition is an imposture. Indeed, if it purports to be God, we can be certain that an imposture is what it is, for if it is comprehended by a finite and individuated consciousness, comprehended in its totality so as to leave no room for doubt as to deception or duplicity, then it is not God, who is infinite and beyond such comprehension. Whereas if it is a representative of God which convinces us, by its (apparent) reality and character, of the transcendent reality of the true God beyond it, how does it relieve our minds of doubt? How does such a condition differ from our present state *vis à vis* the world, where it is argued that the world's reality and character give grounds for a belief in transcendent existence of the true God beyond *it* and yet doubt remains possible as to the truth of such a conclusion as opposed to its alternatives?

Of course, it may be argued that in our future (glorified) state the mind will be relieved through divine grace of its natural propensity to doubt. But this relieving of the mind of its critical capacity sounds more like what might be expected from the action of a psychic drug than from that of a benevolent Deity. And even then the problem is not resolved. For the subjective assurance of certainty is not knowledge, and no matter how the irascible impulse to criticism may be lulled, the gap remains, as long as we are finite beings, between what we know and what we might desire to know. In this sense, it seems, the Bible sums up the human condition in respect to God, not only for our present circumstances but for any circumstances in which the human mind retains its finite human character, when it says 'man shall not see me and live.'

2. Thus the widespread notion that critical thinking requires the substitution of probability for certainty is untenable if by critical thinking is meant radical empiricism.

For radical empiricism can no more impart probable knowledge of the reality of objects outside the mind or their correspondence to appearances than it can impart certainty in their regard.

3. Hence the empiricist critiques of the Cartesian *cogito,* whether in Hobbes, in Hume or in Ayer, are predicated upon the failure to discover the self by the same means we employ in the discovery of a toothache or the taste of sugar in our tea.

4. In *From a Logical Point of View,* Cambridge, 1961.

5. See *The Varieties of Religious Experience: A Study in Human Nature,* New York, 1902.

6. "Über formal unentscheidbare Sätze der *Principia Mathematica* und verwandter Systeme I" *Monatschefte für Mathematik und Physik* XXXVIII (1931), pp. 173-198.

7. *Proslogium,* Preface.

8. Reply to Gaunilon I, tr. S. N. Deane in ST. ANSELM, *Basic Writings,* La Salle, 1903 (2nd ed. 1966), p. 154, or tr. A. B. Wolter (more explicitly for this passage) in *Medieval Philosophy* ed. J. F. Wippel and A. B. Wolter, New York, 1969, p. 163.

9. Thus in the title: "and again of God, that he exists." But even this can be taken in two ways: that a second proof of the existence of God will be offered or that a further discussion of divine existence is intended. Critical evaluation necessitates the second reading unless Descartes is to be presumed to have so sacrificed rigor as to re-demonstrate an established conclusion. This line of inquiry naturally invites comparison of the propositions proved in Meditations 3 and 5—and that can only call attention to the added element, ontic necessity.

It is characteristic of Descartes' approach to his prospective readers' presumptions that he would intentionally promote the former impression although the effectiveness of his argument depends upon his adoption of the latter. Similarly Descartes works hard to give the dramatic impression in the First Meditation that his doubt is all-encompassing, despite his constant awareness, as he writes, of the intuitions which are at no time doubted and by which his systematic, methodical doubt is to be relieved.

10. See Spinoza's *Principles of Descartes' Philosophy,* Part I, prop. xi, for example; and esp. the scholium to prop. v.

11. See *The Guide to the Perplexed* I and my discussion in *RAMBAM,* parts 1 and 2. Descartes' motive, I suspect, for concealing his true object in the Fifth Meditation was plainly the fear of theological persecution or misunderstanding. For to those familiar with the traditions of natural theology it would be evident what followed from the demonstration that God's existence was of the kind called necessary, whereas for the more traditionally inclined, who looked askance upon the outcome of all negative theology, it did not seem amiss to represent the brunt of the Fifth Meditation as simply another demonstration of what had already been proved.

12. Findlay, characteristically, is fully alive to the limitations of his argument: "I admit to the full that my argument *doesn't* hold for those who have no desire to say that God exists in some necessary and inescapable manner. . . . And my argument also *doesn't* hold for those who regard the Ontological Proof (or some other *a priori* proof) as a valid argument. Nor will it hold for those who are willing to say, with Rainer, that one might *come* to perceive the necessity of God's existence in some higher mystical state, nor for those who say, with Hughes and St. Thomas that God himself can perceive the 'necessity' of his own 'existence,' though both this 'existence' and this 'necessity' are something totally different from anything that we understand by these terms. I should indeed be naive if I thought I could trap the analogical eel in my dialectical net. But my argument holds for all those thinkers—who may properly be called 'modern' in no narrow or 'tendentious' sense—who accept Kant's view that there aren't any necessary facts of existence and who can also be persuaded to hold that a God who is 'worth his salt' must either exist necessarily (in the same sense of 'necessary') or not at all." *New Essays in Philosophical Theology,* ed. A. Flew and A. MacIntyre, New York, 1964 (1955), p. 73.

Findlay accurately describes as modern the post-Kantian (or post-Humean) view that there are no necessary facts. But neither he nor Hume nor Kant gives adequate grounds for such a view. The argument from which such a conclusion might be supposed to follow is based upon the fact that alternatives are always conceivable to any experienced state of affairs. But this does not tell us that state of affairs is not necessary but only that we have no grounds in its givenness in experience to presume or infer such a necessity. Indeed a given state of affairs may be necessary without our knowing that, *i.e.,* without our knowing of the causes which may render it necessary. In such a case its contingency would be illusory, a figment of our ignorance. The conceivability of an alternative would be a mere formal or logical virtuality, not a real possibility. Or, in the view of those extreme rationalists who regard the positing of causes (that is of complete causal systems) as implying their effects, even the lack of a formal implication, by which a given effect might be necessitated logically, would be regarded as the result solely of our failure (in our ignorance) to posit sufficient causal grounds and systems of premises to demonstrate the necessity of some effects, the impossibility of others. In this fashion Spinoza upheld the necessity of all events and declared all contingency to be illusory. I can discover no contradiction to the phenomena of experience in this account, nor any violation of the canons of consistency. But, of course, it is not necessary to identify causal with formal necessities nor to agree with the universalization of the rule of necessity and the absolute negation of contingency in order to recognize that (a) the logical possibility of an alternative to a given proposition within a given premise system does not demonstrate the inapplicability of the notion of necessity to the state of affairs that proposition describes and therefore (b) the conceivability of alternative states of affairs to those we experience does not prove their contingency; still less, the contingency of all being.

13. See *Metaphysics* 993b, 19 ff.

14. By a myth, of course, I do not mean an untrue story but rather a story intended to convey some fundamental truth about the nature of reality.

15. The distinction between essence and existence upon which Avicenna's argument was based can be traced back to Aristotle. For Aristotle clearly distinguishes the question as to what a thing is from the question whether a being of such and such a nature exists. Aristotle does not seem to have been aware of the possibility that this distinction between essence and existence might militate against his own desire to equate the "existence" or being of a thing with its essence, that is its being what it is, the kind of thing it is, its membership in its species and instantiation of its form.

In his *History of Christian Philosophy in the Middle Ages* (New York, 1955, p. 186) Étienne Gilson quotes an "important text" in which al-Farabi appears to have anticipated Avicenna in distinguishing essence from existence and treating the latter as a "superadded accident." The text, however, stems from the *Fuṣûs al-Hikam* (ed. Dieterici, Leiden, 1890), a work which S. Pines has shown to be far more likely of later provenance and textually dependent in its entirety on a work of Avicenna's, the *Risâlat ul-Firdaws.* See Pines' article in *Revue des Études Islamiques* 19 (1951), pp. 121-124. I am grateful to Josef Van Ess of Tübingen for enlightening me with regard to this fact.

16. An English translation of Avicenna's argument as stated in his *Kitâb al-'Arsh* is found in A. J. Arberry, ed., *Avicenna On Theology,* London, 1952, pp. 25-27.

17. *Critique of Pure Reason* A598/B626. The translations used here are from Norman Kemp Smith's version, London, 1929, repr. New York, St. Martins, 1965.

18. Far from being a miserable tautology, Maimonides argues that the assertion of the existence of God is a magnificent tautology. It is on these lines that he interprets the Biblical tetragrammaton and God's Self-revelatory phrase—"I am that I am" as expressing the Self-sufficiency of a Necessary Being; *cf.* the discussion in my *RAMBAM,* pp. 100 ff.

19. *Critique of Pure Reason* A598/B626.

20. A599/B627.

21. A600/B628.

22. SPINOZA. *Ethics,* Part I, Definition I, Proposition 7; *cf. Short Treatise* I.

23. *Ethics.* Part I, Definition 8, Proposition 8.

24. Hence his arguments in *De Caelo* and the *Physics* for the eternity of the heavens.

25. It seems strange that this should be so since Aristotle distinguished the question what a thing is from that of whether such a thing exists. Yet the contradiction is inherent in his philosophy—as is evident from the contradiction between the deterministic and indeterministic tendencies in Aristotle's thought. It seemed not only natural but wise to Aristotle to conclude what he regarded as his predecessors' inchoate search for the

"principle" of things' being (or existence) with the discovery of essences as the answer to the problem of existence. But, of course, it could not be said by Aristotle that the essence of things was existence. That would seem to leave the world undifferentiated. Nonetheless, the existence of things for Aristotle (at least in general terms) was necessary. For their existence was their (specific) essences; and these, things had necessarily, by the laws of their own nature. For particulars as such, to put the matter scholastically, existence was *per accidens;* but, as members instantiating a species, necessary. And in the case of the world's "principal parts," the spheres—necessary again. For the contradictions in Aristotle's system, many of which are logically related to the tensions between monism and pluralism and determinism versus contingency, see S. Van Den Bergh, Averroes' *Tahafut al-Tahafut (The Incoherence of the Incoherence),* Volume 2, p. 215, London, 1969.

26. Thomas Aquinas, *Summa Theologica* Question 2, art. 1; see Maimonides, *Guide to the Perplexed* Part I, chapters 1-64, relevant passages translated with commentary in my *RAMBAM.*

27. New data will alter the relative credibility or apparent acceptability of alternative explanations by varying the compatibility of their postulates with accepted assumptions, but new hypotheses are constantly possible and old ones are constantly capable of refurbishment (in sometimes seemingly extravagant but never categorically impossible forms). This holds true equally, symmetrically, with the confirmation and the disconfirmation of hypotheses. Karl Popper wisely recognized that if a proposition cannot be verified conclusively by inductive inference neither can its probability be established inductively, since there may be an infinitude of "confirming" phenomena for a false hypothesis. But Popper imagined that a single countercase might disconfirm a properly formulated (i.e., sufficiently "refutable") hypothesis although it might never conclusively eliminate a particular hypothesis. For observation could contradict the phenomena whose occurrence had been deductively predicted from a given hypothesis. But his last assumption overlooks the possible disparity of phenomena and reality. Hypotheses are speculative conjectures as to the nature of things, and what is deduced from them must be states of affairs in the nature of things. The assumption that such states of affairs will be manifested in observable phenomena demands a metaphysical assumption of the conformance of appearance to reality, which can, of course never be a matter of observation. The notion, then that refutation or disconfirmation is somehow epistemically asymmetrical with verification or confirmation appears to be in error. Moreover, even the refutation of a given hypothesis (say an unmodified, un-elaborated one), if that could be done, does nothing to diminish the set of alternatives: infinitude is not reduced to finitude by any finite series of diminutions.

28. The aesthetic analogue of this position in art is found perhaps in the work of Jackson Pollock, which creates order out of an illusion of disorder. The shunning of (organic) form and (familiar) order and the seeming surrender of the artist's medium and materials to the play of chance create a seeming disorder, and out of that disorder a coherent statement and indeed ultimately a language capable of subtly nuanced statements. But the whole enterprise rests on a paradox—the coherent expression of incoherence, the use of the symbols of disorder for the orderly expression of the varieties of disorder—exactly as positivists use the language of unintelligibility to render experience intelligible and then proceed to discuss the nuanced varieties of unintelligibility.

In art, of course, as in philosophies considered in their purely aesthetic dimension, values arise which may render paradox quite pardonable or even delightful. But, if the intention is to make a statement, as in the case of the positivist philosophers assuredly it is, then the paradox of offering unintelligibility as the universal explanation renders that statement itself necessarily untenable.

29. *Cf.* Saadya Gaon's interpretation of *Ecclesiastes* and my discussion of his pluralism in the *Journal of the American Oriental Society,* forthcoming.

30. In the exordium of his second tractate in the *Book of Beliefs and Opinions,* Saadya writes: "Let me preface this tractate by saying that the data of the sciences are manifest, but their conclusions are abstruse, that they reach some ultimate understanding beyond which there is no understanding, and that a man's improvement in understanding is progressive, each stage necessarily subtler and more abstruse than the last, until the

ultimate stage is reached, at which what is understood is the subtlest and most abstruse of all. Once a man has finally reached that ultimate of subtlety, that is what he was seeking. It is not permissible for him then to try to substitute for the conclusion he has reached something manifest or evident. If he harbors such a hope, then what he wishes for is to return to the original level of understanding at which he started, or to the second, in violation of the basic distinctions of inquiry. Whenever one attempts to place the final object of understanding on the footing of the obvious or manifest, one only vitiates one's own thought process, or rather nullifies his understanding altogether and reverts to the same state of ignorance with which he started.'' I have translated this passage myself because, I fear, the standard published version is seriously in misleading on several counts. What Saadya means, as he explains in the paragraphs that follow, is that with respect to general explanations of nature we begin with data which are evident *(jalîla)* because they are sensory. To explain these, we resort to theories whose terms are abstract as we might put it. But Saadya avoids the use of such a word, which might suggest the negation of concreteness, *i.e.,* of reality. Rather he uses the words *latîf,* abstruse and *altafu,* more abstruse (and *adiqqu,* subtler), by which he means further removed from the sensory and thus, in Platonic terms, more akin to the intellectual (and so to the more real)—closer ultimately to some object of understanding for which there is no subsequent or ulterior explanation *(ma'lûm akhîr fa-lâ yakûn warâ'ahu ma'lûm akhar).* To expect of this ultimate explanatory term that it exhibit the same evidence as the sensory terms with which we began is to violate the rules of the game, that is to forget that it was only by reversion to a more highly abstruse level *(i.e.,* the level of things thought and understood rather than that of things seen) that any understanding was achieved at all. Even if we were to succeed somehow in rendering our final object of understanding evident *(e.g.,* to the eyes, the fingers or the nose) we should only have succeeded in vitiating all the preceding thought process, by which understanding had been reached, and revert to our original state of ignorance, that is the contemplation of an unexplained (sense) datum.

III

MONOTHEISM AND ETHICS

Like all other forms of explanation or elements referred to in explanations, the notion we have of the existence of God is a fiction. By this I do not mean that it is false to assert the existence of God. Quite the contrary, I have endeavored to show the grounds on which that existence may be affirmed as a necessary truth. But the very idea of a Being whose existence is necessary is a truth which far transcends our comprehension. That is how it is possible, as Aquinas explained in glossing "The fool hath said in his heart there is no God," that a fact which is necessary in itself may appear so dubious to us and how it is possible, as Saadya put it, for that by which all else is explained to be the most abstruse of all conceptions, the least readily related to the ordinary data of experience.

Through the concept of God we can integrate experience and consummate the progress of rationalism by bringing explanation to the point of self-explanatory unity, allowing God's absolute and infinite perfection to stand in place of any surds at which an uncompleted rationalism might be tempted to abandon itself in the positivism which would trivialize all its understanding. No one understood this fact better than Einstein, who relied upon that understanding in his efforts to create an alternative to the scientific positivism which he felt sure was the undoing of all scientific inquiry, as I hope to show in a study of the philosophic elements of Einstein's cosmology.

For us, from our human standpoint, the existence of God can be affirmed (as it was by the ancient prophets) as the hypothesis which completes the pattern of our understanding of nature and of values— God as the Primal Cause and Ultimate Good, an hypothesis which for us has no certainty, but which, as monotheists, we find to be confirmed by experience. God is a fiction in the same sense that π is a fiction, or gravity or causality. But unlike some of these concepts, God's concept involves reality, and that of an absolute sort, and no particularity but universality, absolute perfection. And for that reason all the best that we can say anent God is on a par with the stories which we tell the children, which we may dignify with the name of poetry, or if it seems to express truth, of revelation, speaking from the perspective then of God, ignoring our groping activity and presuming all valid insight to spring from His Self-revelatory action, sensing that alongside the dynamic of the Absolute all finite activity is passivity, and in the case of our prophets and ecstatics, surrendering to that passivity once the authenticity of the divine dynamic has been accepted.

But if it is an absolute and infinitely transcendent Being we speak of, what possible bearing could It have on our lives: (i.) Can the mere existence of a Being have any moral relevance? Antony Flew, long a valuable gadfly of natural theology (although he has labored to far too great an extent under the impression that Catholicism is the only theological system worthy of his essays at refutation[1]) argued pointedly in *God and Philosophy* that "we cannot deduce any normative conclusion from premises which are all neutrally descriptive."[2] (ii.) Assuming that the existence of an absolute being can be conceived to involve ethical imperatives, there is, it seems, no way of specifying those imperatives. From a transcendental, universal premise, how can a concrete and particular conclusion be derived? Arguing *a propos* of the Catholic prudential suasion that a life other than that demanded or expected by God will be requited with eternal punishment, Flew wrote: "Pascal's Roman Catholicism threatens with endless torture all those outside the true mystical body of Christ. But it is just as conceivable that there is a hidden God (Pascal's own "Deus absconditus"!) who will consign all and only Catholics to the fate they [or some of them along with some Protestants as well] so easily approve for others. Since there is an unlimited range of pairs of possible transcendental religious systems, threatening as well as encouraging every conceivable way of life— including every variety of agnosticism and incredulity—with exactly the same inordinate rewards and punishments, such transcendentally backed threats cannot provide even a prudential reason for choosing one way of life rather than another."[3]

The reasoning here, unfortunately is a bit facile. Flew's discovery of a plurality of religious/ethical options is belated and does not allow him to consider the possibility that a universal and, therefore, exclusivist theology need not be condemnatory.[4] Moreover, the conclusion that what is required of man by a transcendental and hidden God is obscure or arbitrary is reached too hastily. God, as a perfect being, might be obscure to us while at the same time what we may with some propriety regard as the "divine will" is not obscure at all. There is no contradiction in that.

The reliance upon prudential suasions as a sufficient font of ethics is easily discredited. It would be a poor, mean ethics—or rather an ethic of poor-spiritedness and meanness, which is to say no ethic at all—which was founded on the fear of sanctions, even infinite sanctions ascribed to some fabular emotion of divine displeasure. But if it is ethics we are searching for within the concept of divinity (and that is the very meaning and birthright of religion, which is not merely some system of theology but—as we learn from Epicurus—the endeavor to regulate human life in accordance with what we take to be the true conception of divinity), then the questions remain: How can fact (given that the existence of God is fact) legislate value? How can the Transcendent Absolute, whose very conception in our minds is at best a lofty and abstruse ideal, regulate the particularities of the here and now?

Added to these two problems there is a third which was most clearly articulated by Kant: morality as such requires freedom as its necessary (and, Kant believed, sufficient) condition. Freedom must be understood, Kant held, as autonomy, not merely the opportunity for choice, but the positive presence of self-legislation. But if the moral law is legislated on divine authority, heteronomy, the rule of something other than the self, is substituted for the rule of the rational will (Kantian self) and morality is lost. Quite apart from any question of sanctions or pressures, morality without autonomy, the free self-legislation of the law by the rational will, is a contradiction in terms. And this defect, that is the endeavor to legislate morality out of the authority of a divine legislator, in Kantian thinking vitiates every sort of communal or organized religion, every notion that the very concept of divinity may impose obligations. Epicurus stated the same argument in even broader terms. Where Kant was to treat action on the pleasure principle as heteronomous, Epicurus, identifying the true pleasure principle with the rational will argued that not only no divinity but no transcendental (non-sensory) ideal was a legitimate (i.e., freely chosen, hence properly moral) standard of morality. Even the Kantian ideal of duty (a secularized, personalized, de-divinized transcendental standard) would by this criterion fail by its very transcendental character as a legitimate foundation of morality.

Three questions then must be asked of any religious approach to ethics: (i) How, if at all can "facts legislate values?" (ii) How can the abstract and universal be read as specifying the concrete and particular? (iii) How can any standard of morality outside the confines of the in-dividual personality be regarded as imposing obligations without the loss of freedom (autonomy), which is an essential mark of the moral sphere as such? These are the questions which must be answered in behalf of monotheism, and it is noteworthy at the outset that the answers which are appropriate in the case of monotheism are not identical with those which naturally suggest themselves in the case of non-monotheistic theological schemes.

(i)

The problem of facts and values has long been recognized as central to morals. Hume wrote of the disparity he found in works on ethics which seemed to make a strange transition from the realm of is to that of ought. How can merely existential premises yield conclusions which are prescriptive in force? Where have the syntactic operators necessary to prescription entered in?[5] G. E. Moore used his open question method to demonstrate that the concept of 'good' is not definable in naturalistic terms and hence not deducible from merely factual premises. For whenever 'good' is equated with some natural property or item, the question of the adequacy of the analysis remains open, as would be impossible if the analysis were adequate. Moore was at pains to apply the results of this analysis to the refutation of theological subjectivism and indeed all theologically deduced systems of ethical obligation: "To hold that from any proposition asserting 'Reality is of this nature' we can infer, or obtain confirmation for any proposition asserting 'This is good in itself' is to commit the naturalistic fallacy. And that a knowledge of what is real supplies reasons for holding certain things to be good in themselves is either implied or expressly asserted by all those who define the Supreme Good in metaphysical terms."[6] Flew, with notable precision, states that no normative or prescriptive conclusion can be derived from merely neutral statements of fact.

Here I think we find the two sources of the problem. For (1.) the monotheistic assertion of the existence of God is not the assertion of a mere, brute or "neutral" fact. Nor, indeed, is it an assertion about the natural world or any natural properties or items: although it is founded on investigation of the world, it involves a conclusion which reaches infinitely beyond the world. Moreover, (2.) Moore erred in supposing that the derivation of ethical obligations from the fact of divine existence is necessarily some type of deductive or inductive inference or any type of detached propositional calculation. Hume had fallen into the same error when he allowed himself to wonder whence sprang the moral, practical force of ethical sentiments if they were mere inferential derivatives of descriptive statements.[7] The source of the error is the post-Cartesian tendency to color all aspects of experience cognitively as a result of the philosophic preeminence assigned to epistemology. Thus in the very process of recognizing the non-indicative status of ethical judgments,

Hume permits himself to picture as anomalous their relationship to matters of fact.

The monotheistic concept of God is the concept of a Being of absolute perfection, and the statement of the existence of that being cannot be regarded as the statement of a neutral fact. Rather, the assertion 'God is' is the equivalent of the claim that 'Goodness is,' provided it is understood that the affirmation is of a Reality and of no mere abstraction and understood that no humanly limited conception of goodness can be substituted for this conception of perfect Goodness.

In terms of this analysis the whole question of theistic subjectivism is revealed, monotheistically, to be a pseudo-question. It is unintelligible to inquire whether what is right is such because it is the will of God or vice versa, for by God's will the philosophic monotheist who is careful with his concepts can mean nothing other than what is right; and, vice versa, by what is right, a monotheistic thinker whose reasoning holds its concepts constant can mean nothing other than "God's will" so far as it is intelligible to us.

The famous open question method in this case does not apply. For when it is assumed that what is desired by God may conceivably be at variance with what is right so that the equation of the two notions is called into question and the adequacy of the analysis refuted, it is only by the substitution for the monotheistic conception of God of some other concept in which God is held to be less than perfect. The open question argument, if applied in the case of strict, conceptually disciplined monotheism commits the fallacy of equivocation.[8]

Of course, the fact that there exists a God who is absolute perfection does not by itself imply that there are obligations. The Humean gap between 'is' and 'ought' remains. But then no statement and no fact *by itself* implies anything, as we have seen. There must be a context, and part of the context relevant with regard to obligations is that there must be subjects for them. It is in this sense that traditional monotheism has understood creation, as affording a milieu or context for the fulfillment of the obligations stemming from the Divine. But still the gap remains— as pictured in the dramatic focal point of the Sistine ceiling—between the divine 'I am' and the human 'ought.' For no is can *imply* an ought.

Yet implication is not the only possible relation, nor even the appropriate relation, for obligations are not implied, except by other obligations in the same sort of hypothetical scheme by which judgments may be formally regarded as implied by other judgments. Obligations are imposed, or as it is expressed in the scintillating metaphor of the Mosaic code, they are commanded. Creation itself is regarded as taking place by commandment and ultimately in a way for the sake of commandment— else God's Self-sufficiency, it is reasoned, would have sufficed to Itself.

And commandment is a primal mode of (symbolic) intercourse between the monotheistic God and human creation in particular.

The very existence of a Being of Absolute Perfection involves obligations, not in and of itself but in the context of the experience of finite beings such as ourselves, capable of grasping the concept of such a being and feeling the claim that concept makes on us. If God exists, then we are bound, not logically but morally, to strive for all that is best in ourselves and best in others. This does not, of course, imply that if (*per impossibile*) God does not exist there are no other ways of seeking justification for comparable obligations.

We are not saying that obligation is the arbitrary fiat of divine will, without which no obligation would exist. Quite the contrary, the very concept of a divine will has no meaning relative to the human condition except by reference to such ideas as those of good, right, moral obligation, and other notions expressive of positive values. To be sure, if there were no God there would be no values, for there would be nothing. But the supposition (of the Biblical fool) that there is no God does not imply (as Alyosha feared in *The Brothers Karamazov*) that "everything is permitted." For the God whose nonexistence is conceivable is not the real God, but a fabular figment or imagined surrogate of God. The denial of the reality of the being so imagined, of course does not imply (*per impossibile*) the denial of all values (as would the denial of the God in whom all perfections are comprised), but only a kind of fragmentation or reversion to paganism, in which value is located in particulars but not integrated in a Monadic Source. Here too there would be obligations, albeit hypothetical only. But since the force of hypothetical imperatives (or judgments of relative value) rests on that of the categorical imperative (applied intuition of absolute value) there is always the possibility of the reconstruction of morals, whether confusedly, without the thought of the Integral Source of all value, or clearly, with that thought. The "death of God" in the confused imagination is never a final death of God for humanity because morality can always right itself and regenerate theology by the same dialectic of values and their critique which first generated monotheism and its ethic. Thus contrary to the once widespread notion, ethical behavior does not presuppose religious belief, but all ethical (and other) value does nevertheless stem from God. And so the existence of God imposes ethical obligations, not in the abstract but in relation to any being capable of aspiration towards what it conceives as highest and best.

Recognition of the fact that the relation of perfection to aspiration is not one of implication but one of command (*mitzvah*) should be sufficient to clear up one of the most widespread misconceptions among aspirants to philosophy, the notion that there is some insoluble paradox (or plain falsehood) in the Socratic dictum 'To know the good is to do good.' If this assertion is taken to state a relation of implication or equivalence, counterexamples are readily produced. There are of course many individuals who "know" abstractly and can state what actions under given circumstances would be right, but fail to perform accordingly. Yet to treat such cases as countercases to the Socratic dictum is, as Plato teaches us, to fail to accord full seriousness to the idea of knowing the good.

To know the good in the fullest sense is to recognize or intuit the absoluteness of divine perfection. Is such an experience compatible with unethical behavior? Abstractly speaking it seems so. Morally speaking it is not. The recognition of the absolute perfection of divinity is fraught with moral significance for an aspiring being. It imposes a moral imperative on such a being consciously to seek perfection (just as it imposes a natural necessity on non-conscious beings to pursue their perfection by the avenues open to them). Conscious action is voluntary. It may seek to deny or reject the imperative it senses, partially or totally, choosing a distorted image of perfection or rejecting the very notion of pursuing perfection. And in this sense moral behavior is not automatic among conscious beings even when they have some glimmer of the idea of Perfection. But the feeling or hearing of the imperative toward perfection, to be obeyed or disobeyed, is the inevitable consequence of confrontation between an aspiring being and a being of absolute perfection.

Such confrontation may be shunned or evaded, its impact not appropriated to one's personhood, or distorted, diminished, or minimized. It is for this reason, I believe, that we tend to regard persons whom we suppose to have sufficient intellectual grounds for the formation of an adequate moral stance as suffering from a moral flaw (e.g. hypocrisy) rather than an intellectual one. But the moral claim upon aspiring beings is to seek in themselves for that perfection which they encounter outside themselves. In this sense (although there is many a slip) to know the good is to do good—that is to recognize perfection is to feel its command toward the appropriation of perfection as the ordering principle of all lesser goals. And taking 'knowledge' in a more integrated (and more Platonic) sense than that of purely academic apprehension, as referring to the principles of action one has incorporated in one's character, there would indeed be a paradox in saying that someone knew what was right but did not do it.

When I speak of obligation in terms of mitzvah and of mitzvah in terms of obligation there is an appearance of circularity which ought to be cleared up. Mitzvah phenomenologically is (primally) the prophetic awareness of a moral fact as an objective moral datum, the objectivity expressed as the issuance of that datum from the mouth of God. The same fact can be viewed subjectively, i.e. from a human perspective, and then it is, phenomenologicaly, the experience of the moral appropriation of the right course or type of course in one's own character. The sages call this appropriation assumption of the yoke of the kingdom of Heaven—that is the onus of obligation under the laws of the universal Imperium, a typical challenge in their language to the limited authority of the earthly Imperium of Caesar. Or the same moral fact or datum may be expressed in relation to a third party, as a matter of right. There is on this account no distinction to be made except that of perspective between saying ' ϕ is what ought to be done,' ' ϕ is right,' 'I have an obligation to act so as to see that ϕ is done,' 'X has a right that ϕ be done,' and ' ϕ is God's will.' The Hebrew usage expresses an awareness of this in- terchangeability of moral perspectives in its reliance upon the idea of justice (*tzedakkah*) rather than that of right or duty as the central concept of the Biblical system of morals/law. For the term *justice* can be substituted generically for each occurrence of ϕ in the preceding schemata, as can any instance of right action.

The moral datum is a fundamental fact, a fact which can be recognized inchoately without explicit reference to the concept of divine commands. So there need be no fear of circularity in describing obligations as mitzvot and mitzvot as obligations, for it is possible to ascertain a content for human obligations without explicit reference to the idea of divinity and thus it is not the case that the content of those obligations need be "derived" from knowledge of the divine commands while the latter are deduced from the former. On the contrary, we have primary awareness of what the canons of perfection require of us—a precognitive awareness, even, it might be said, since all beings, even non-conscious beings in their own ways, pursue their own good insofar as it is open to them. The dependence of values on God is ontic, not logical; and the making explicit of the nature of that dependence is the perquisite of religion, not the prerequisite of ethics. Religion may perfect morality (or pervert it) but is hardly necessary on our account to morality's discovery. Morality can originate in personal grievance or social tact. The per- fection of its logic as a self-conscious system of goals depends on monotheism; surely not the first glimmerings of perception of those goals.

The concept for which the Biblical metaphor of commandment (*mitzvah*) stands symbolically, then, is that of a demand for recognition on the part of man of an obligation to seek fulfillment of the human aspiration toward perfection. This recognition is an event or sequence of events in the human mind, but it comes naturally in the idiom of radical monotheism adopted Biblically to express it (as all else) as an act of God.

In terms of monotheism there is no objective distinction between its being the one or the other. (But, of course, there is no contingency in the divine "will" or "act." This simply means the manifestation of the divine Reality to human consciousness—in this case, human moral consciousness.) There is, therefore, no question of a naturalistic fallacy between the divine fact and the imposition of moral values arising from the recognition of that fact. For Divinity is not simply another "neutral" fact but the totality of all value. And the relation posited is not one of logical implication but of moral invocation, dependent on the openness to the concept of transcendent perfection being present in beings capable of response. Just as in grammar there is no imperative without an understood subject, so here, the divine imperative is not the abstract implication of a fact but the very intimate (or public) invocation which an idea as possibility or actuality makes to a mind and will, or as the Bible puts it, symbolizing the unity of mind and will by a single term, to a heart.

(ii)

The issue of eschatology as a sanction of morality is easily shown to be a red herring not only morally but also theologically, from the monotheistic point of view. The Jewish sages picture both the blessed and the damned seated in long rows opposite one another in the World to Come. Before them a feast is laid, but both the blessed and the damned have their arms bound in splints and can do nothing to put the delicacies into their mouths. Where then is the difference? The wretched suffer agonies in their inability to enjoy the feast. But among the righteous each feeds his neighbor opposite and all take joy not only in the feast but in the joy they give to others.

The error in Flew's homily, which he takes to be argument, is in his supposition that what God commands, if God is transcendent, is an arbitrary matter subject to an infinitude of viewpoints and perspectives. This would be true if it were a pagan deity we were speaking of. For every pagan (or particular) god is only the projection of a particular value or value complex, which can be celebrated or defined only by its contrast with (and violation of) other conflicting values. The monotheistic God is the integration of all values, and hence there is no ambiguity in what that God requires.

The notion that human standards of morality are widely different is a well-known shibboleth of pluralistic cant. In fact the core human notions of decency and rectitude vary but little from culture to culture and then only in response to pressing situational factors or the vested interests and demands of some class or ideology. Most moral differences (as opposed to the familiar apologetics of self-serving cant) are differences of strategy or style rather than differences of principle—and thus in the strict sense are not moral differences at all.

It is possible, of course, for a culture or an ethos as for an individual to become demoralized in conditions of severe asperity or through moral unpreparedness for affluence. There is cultural decadence, and there is as well a kind of psychic defense strategy by which cruelty, pain and death are confronted, *faute de mieux,* with a kind of gallows humor or even transmuted into positive values, as a result of the mind's deepseated unwillingness to accept evil as such. In the utmost reaches of tribal penury, one reads that death becomes a joke. And in the Nazi death camps, it is said that values took on strangely distorted forms. But even in these circumstances, under the most extreme imaginable of conditions, values universally recognizable as representing the highest levels of human nobility and courage reassert themselves. We are conditioned, not determined by our surroundings.

The East (or any exotic land) is the traditional referent of arguments as to the widespread variation of human moral standards. The reason, of course, is the superficially exotic character of the customs of nations other than our own and the prevalence of social systems which have the effect of assigning divergent significance to what we imagine to be the same actions in diverse cultural contexts. But the language and the basis as well as the outcome of moral discourse remain constant. The same story I have told as to the righteous and the wicked with their arms in splints is told also in the orient. The difference is that the saints and wretches have been provided with chopsticks too long to reach their own mouths.

Cannibals, the favorite recourse of those who seek some important means of refuting what they take to be moral dogmatism, do not eat men because they think it morally right to do so but because they have not seen as yet the need to purge their notion of divinity of that ritualized *frisson* associated with the violation of humanity and symbolized in the devouring of brains or hearts or marrow bones (or, alternatively, allegedly because their diet requires protein). Custom can habituate and institutions rationalize virtually any practice. Cannibals are not alone, of course, as victims of the tyranny of usage. The important point is not that we can become so accustomed to any usage as to feel ready to defend it but that we are, it seems to me, universally capable of recognizing the flaws in our own customs. Thus we are amenable to moral insight, communication and instruction.

When Albert Schweitzer first set up his medical station at Lambaréné, one of the tribal peoples he was treating was a cannibal group, the Pahouins. He noted their custom and their general aggressiveness as well as their tendency to lie and steal. One can see that he wondered whether and in what way his work and teaching might prove a moral influence on them. But Schweitzer turns out to have been the learner. When World War I broke out, recruits were taken from the area. Weeks later word came back that ten of these recruits were dead. It was the cannibals who were shocked: " 'Ten men killed already in this war!' said an old Pahouin. 'Why, then, don't the tribes meet for a palaver? How can they pay for all these dead men?' "⁹ The level of human waste taken for granted in mechanized warfare among modern nations and made possible (some would say necessary) by a high level of social integration was inconceivable to the cannibals. They had no lack of understanding of the idea of human worth, although some of their society's institutions were predicated upon its ritual flouting (and others upon the assignment to it of a nominal monetary price)—no more than Schweitzer lacked that concept, although the culture which had borne him, and to which he bore allegiance in many but not all ways, flouted it far more systematically.

George Catlin, the great American painter who travelled among the Indians of North America to document their culture and create portraits of their leading personalities recorded an occasion he observed of the exposure of an elderly tribesman no longer able to travel with the group—another favorite instance of those who claim that moral standards differ widely from culture to culture:

> When we were about to leave the village of the Puncahs we found that they too were packing up all their goods . . . My attention was directed to one of the most miserable and helpless-looking objects I have ever seen in my life: a very aged and emaciated man of the tribe, who was to be *exposed*.
>
> The tribe were going where hunger compelled them to go. The old man, who had once been a chief and a man of distinction in the tribe, was now too old to travel. He was reduced to mere skin and bones. He was to be left to starve, or meet with such death as might fall to his lot, and his bones to be picked by the wolves . . .
>
> His eyes were dimmed. His venerable locks were whitened by a hundred years. His limbs were almost naked. He trembled as he sat by a small fire which his friends had left him, with a few sticks of wood within his reach and a buffalo's skin stretched upon some crotches over his head. It was to be his only dwelling, and his chances for life were reduced to a few half-picked bones laid within his reach, and a dish of water. He was without weapon of any kind to replenish his supply, or strength to move his body from its fatal locality.
>
> He had unluckily outlived the fates and accidents of wars to die alone at death's leisure. His friends and his children had all left him and were preparing to be on the march. He had told them to leave him: "I am old," he said, "and too feeble to march."
>
> "My children," said he, "our nation is poor, and it is necessary that you should all go to the country where you can get meat. My eyes are dimmed and my strength is no more. My days are nearly all numbered, and I am a burden to my children. I cannot go and I wish to die. Keep

your hearts stout, and think not of me. I am no longer good for anything."
They finished the ceremony of *exposing* him and took their final leave of him.[10]

The feelings here portrayed are the same we would expect in any such human confrontation of unhappy necessity. Clearly only the absence of a viable alternative provides the setting for the choice taken, and if an alternative were available, that choice would not be made a norm. The sensitivity of the ritual formulation to the feelings of those who travel on, the need to free them of guilt, to the extent possible, are clearly indicative of a cultural expectation of universal abhorrence for the act which culturally is regarded as inevitable. Thus it is not the case that Indians or Eskimos or other nomadic people think it "perfectly fine and proper" to abandon their infirm along the road. Quite the contrary, they feel much the same about it as we would feel if it were a type of choice against whose periodic adoption our culture were to provide no insulation. It is not unclear, then, what morality requires of us, although circumstances may restrict the realm in which our moral choices must be made and culture, in response to circumstances (whether objective as with nomad tribes or subjective as with the beliefs and emotions upon which ritual cannibalism is instituted) may modify or deflect the practice through which apprehension of moral norms can be expressed.

The argument of the sages, which they couch as a homily as to the Hereafter shows three things: (a) It illustrates their universal dictum that all is in the hands of Heaven save only the fear of Heaven—for here beatitude depends on our freely adopted (but not so easily escaped) choice of attitude. (b) It demonstrates the triviality of eschatology and the ease with which we each make our own heaven or hell out of the materials of *this* life, specifically out of pleasure and pain. (c) It illuminates quite clearly the simplicity of the nexus between the God of monotheism and the principles of morality, very much in the spirit of Micah (6:8): "It hath been told thee, O man, what is good and what the Lord expects of thee [note the verb: *doresh,* which has a pedagogic force, *i.e.,* not what God compels or even imposes on you—still less what the Divine "implies" but what God teaches and instructs you to do], only to practice justice, to love kindness and decently to walk with thy God." I call the parable of the sages an argument because its soundness (for example, as a piece of theodicy) depends on its verisimilitude to life and its faithfulness to the monotheistic conception of divine transcendence. Flew's intended argument that God might require anything of man and hence there is no telling just what form of behavior is the will of God, I call a homily because it contains no attempt at verisimilitude to the human condition and grossly misrepresents the critical monotheistic conception of God, in which there can be no fault or imperfection (Psalm 92 *ad fin.*); and surely, therefore, no imperative toward any but the most upright form of behavior.

If the question is, 'How could the Infinite and Timeless prescribe laws for the finite and timebound?' the only possible answer within the monotheist framework is 'How could It not?' The very concept of divinity from its origin is bound up with that of what is best and most perfect in a human scale. And the conceptual refinements of the idea of divinity go hand in hand with the refinements in human ethical thinking—above all with the purgation of violence and all forms of evil from the sphere of positive value and so from that of divinity. When the Stoics argue that the divine will must surely be made known to man, they predicate their argument on their own conception of adherence to moral duty as the sole human good. And when the Epicureans argue that moral legislation is no function of the divine, they predicate their rejection of divine governance of man and nature on the premise that such a task is beneath the dignity of what is blessed and immortal. Even the Epicurean gods in their sublime detachment (*ataraxia*) are held worthy of emulation, although divine emulation is not supposed to be the motive for the pursuit of *ataraxia,* which ought rather to be recognized as (the) good in itself and the self-sufficing goal of all desire. But then is not love of goodness for its own sake the central message of monotheism and the identity of that love with the love of God for its own sake the central teaching of monotheistic ethics?

The derivation of morality from the concept of divinity is the least problematic of all conceptual transitions. For it is from our highest and best moral concepts that the concept of divinity takes its rise. It would be a poor thinker indeed who was unable to rederive morality from the Ideal which has morality as its source. The emulation called for by the very contemplation of the concept of divine perfection—expressed Biblically as the human pursuit of holiness (*Leviticus* 19) and in Plato as the striving to become as like to God as lies in human capacity (*Theaetetus* 176)—means simply the pursuit of the highest conceivable moral standards. If there is any problem, it is not in the notion that what God requires is moral decency and rectitude, a proper comportment toward God and man and a striving after human perfection, but rather in the specification of the precise nature of that morality. And this is properly not a theological problem at all but a problem of human moral inquiry.

Plainly the specification required if the divine imperative is to become a law of human action is not performed at the level of the divine. For what we mean when saying God is infinite is that there is no specification of the Divine. But this does not imply that the needed specification is impossible, for that specification can be performed and is performed, as it must be, at the human level. The task of interpreting the concrete requirements commanded or imposed by God is a human task, just as the very notion of a divine will is a human notion. The concept of divinity gives no more than the direction, *i.e.*, the orientation toward the highest good. Even that orientation has no meaning in itself but only with reference to the striving of finite beings, and no moral application, no force as a command, except with reference to beings like ourselves capable of conscious aspiration. The rules it ordains for our behavior it is upon us to discover to the best of our ability. The extent to which such rules can be specific or even particular is a problem we must work out for ourselves. But regardless of the degree to which the moral rules are made specific or even particular, they introduce no specificity or particularity into the nature of the Divine. For all that they derive from the divine is the imperative status of moral rules, *i.e.*, the demand exercised by what is best upon the rational will of all aspiring beings that it be the best which is pursued.

It is sometimes claimed that if God is a being of unique perfection and infinitely transcendent of our comprehension, the specification of the ethical principles which may be deemed to be imposed by reference to the thought of God is necessarily an arbitrary action on the part of human minds. If God is infinitely transcendent, we can make no inferences as to what human actions would be congruent with the divine nature and which, if any, would be incongruent with it.[11] Thus one cannot both concur with Isaiah in the belief that God is transcendent (holy, in the prophet's language) and unique and fulfill the commandment of *Leviticus* (19:2), "Ye shall be holy, for I the Lord thy God am holy," where holiness is given a moral and spiritual meaning as applied to man, involving human self-transcendence and development in the direction of God. Taken this way, theistic transcendentalism is seen to be the source of the "death of God." That is, the fading of the idea of the moral relevance of theism is predicated directly upon the notion that divine transcendence renders human emulation of God impossible.

Alternatively it may be claimed that the transcendence of God demands the adoption of a relativistic conception of moral standards, the idea of God functioning in monotheistic moral schemes as does the idea of emptiness in Buddhism as a kind of touchstone against which exaggerated claims in behalf of specific values can be tested. From the perspective of infinitude, the claims of finitude appear nugatory and the differences among them tend to recede into triviality. *All* have some claim to a share in the Absolute, but none can make good an absolute claim.[12]

If by this is meant that in a given situation there may be more than one optimal moral strategy, that seems self-evident, although one does not need theistic or any other absolutes (such as nothingness or death, etc.) to recognize that possibility. But if by relativism is meant that there is never a situation in which one moral strategy is objectively superior to others or that in no situation are there any objective grounds for setting aside the claims of *any* values in deference to those of others, then the claim is plainly false. The possibility of diverse viewpoints is itself predicated on the recognition of objective merit in diverse value claims, and it would be inconsistent to make that recognition and then hold *a priori* that in no situation could the merit of one case exceed that of another. The idea of the infinitude of God does not imply moral relativism in the sense now specified but rather legislates an obligation of endeavor towards perfection; and, if our perceptions of perfection differ, then towards perfection as we most adequately and objectively perceive it. The analogy which represents all human values and concerns as receding to insignificance from the perspective of infinitude is faulty, for it presupposes a finite rather than infinite Viewer. It is from our perspective as finite, sentient beings that distance involves recession; and moral distance, loss of moral significance. *Vis à vis* the Infinite there is no loss of moral worth and so no retreat of values into insignificance or parity. This, perhaps, is part of what is meant by the formulation (based on the rejection of human moral myopia) describing divine activity as a circle whose center is everywhere.

As for the notion that divine transcendence renders the morality to be derived from the idea of God unspecifiable in view of the divine transcendence, it is predicated on the false assumption that we know nothing of the direction of divine transcendence, whereas, in fact, as we have seen, the logic of the concept of God requires us to locate divine transcendence solely in the direction of perfection. The result is that we can specify quite precisely what "the Lord requireth" of us, to the extent that we are aware of the right moral course to follow. So confident were the Sages of this fact that they did not hesitate to specify quite concretely which (experiential) aspects of God man was to emulate and which, by implication, he was not: As He is holy, so be ye holy, as He is merciful, so be ye merciful, etc.—but not 'As He is impersonal, so be ye impersonal' or 'As He is all-encompassing, so be ye all-encompassing.'[13] This specification of the human task was accomplished not arbitrarily but in accordance with the principle that God's transcendence is transcendence in perfection. So the principles we are called upon to perfect in ourselves by way of *emulatio Dei* are those which are perfections in us, that is, the human virtues.

I wish to return to this issue of the specification of the moral law shortly, no longer as a problem of the nexus of a universal God with a specific code, since I believe that question now is answered, but as a problem in its own right within the sphere of religious ethics, for I wish to reflect upon the Biblical approach to the resolution of that problem as a human approach to the general human problem of specifying and particularizing the universal imperative stemming from perfection itself, and perhaps to some extent to compare and contrast that human approach with certain other human approaches to the same problem. But before I take up that question it remains to settle the third of the issues with which we began, the Kantian (and later Nietzschean) issue of heteronomy, and this I think is fairly easy, now that the proper analysis has been given of the notion of legislation from the divine.

(iii)

The divine imperative is not an external event, not an occasion outside the human mind but an event within the mind itself. To moderns the Biblical imagery may be somewhat misleading in this regard, for it seems to represent the giving of the Law and Covenant in the manner of some ancient public legislation rite and oathing ceremony. As though God were standing here on some lofty or mountainous dais, the people here below, Moses in between, God announcing, the people hearing and swearing to accept what God presents, Moses serving as interlocutor. Yet, as with all the metaphoric imagery of the Bible, the crucial points are made by the departures from the familiar scenes and images. God does not simply stand, for God cannot be seen, Moses does not simply relate, for certain things must be heard directly, and the people do not simply swear allegiance, despite the importance of the concept of the consent of the governed here—or because of it—they are told that they are standing in the place of all future generations of Israel. How can they consent for future generations? What is it that Moses cannot tell them but they must hear for themselves?

What they must hear for themselves is the divine Self-Proclamation 'I am.' What this means to them in concrete terms as an imperative can be conveyed by Moses, but the underlying insight into the concept of divinity each man and woman must fathom for himself and herself to the best of their ability.[14] For it is this concept which imposes on the aspiring will the general imperative to pursue that which is best. This awakening is not something which can be brought about by another, it must come from within, although instruction and the unfolding of culture and history may prepare the ground for it. It is for this reason that the generation of Sinai can stand before God in the symbolic place of all future generations. They cannot accept the most general obligation in behalf of others, but all others must stand precisely in their place, must see it for themselves to the best of their ability, and then endeavor with the aid of tradition and their own best lights to make out its concrete implications in their situations. When this is done, there is no heteronomy. God does not stand apart and impose morality. 'Thou shalt' does not come first, but first 'I am,' and (not by logic but by the dialectic of moral response) 'Thou shalt' follows, now *identical* with 'I will,' since it arises not from culture or tradition or any external source of legislation but from the inward experience of moral appropriation which forms the very identity of the moral personality in those who experience it.

Viewed from the human perspective, the correlative of the divine mitzvah or imperative is expressed Biblically by reference to the metaphor of God and His responding creature as Lover and beloved. That is the human response to mitzvah is *ahavah,* love. Thus human love of God is given as the universal motive for observance of the commandments (*Deuteronomy* 11:1, etc.); and this love is expected to be absolute, that is unconditional.

We are told that we must love God "with all thy heart, with all thy soul and with all thy might." (*Deuteronomy* 6:5). This cannot mean that the thought of God, as in some extreme forms of monism, is to be the sole focus of our attention and concern to the exclusion of all that might be distinguished or differentiated from Him. For the admonition to love God is repeatedly coupled with that of following the commandments. Active observance of the mitzvot is presented as the means by which the love of God is expressed—hence that love itself is represented as the motive for activities conceptually distinguishable from it. The absoluteness of the love of God is transferred to the steadfastness with which observance is to be kept.

The reasoning, I suspect, is that allegiance to God (and hence to the commandments) must not be contingent upon any good fortune associated with that allegiance but must be absolute. For the mitzvot are not mere prudential counsels, although it may be prudent to observe them. They are expressions of a categorical imperative. Yet even pragmatically it is all the more crucial to adhere to the right in times of misfortune if the laws of justice and mutual aid are to confer their pragmatic benefits. Thus the dictum of Antigonos of Socho: "Be not as servants who serve the master for the sake of a reward but be as servants who serve the master not for the sake of a reward (*Avot* 1:3). Antigonos does not say that there is and can be no benefit in faithful adherence to the principles of the mitzvot, nor that we should have no regard to such benefits but only that such benefits should not be that for the sake of which we act, *e.g.* the determining condition sine qua non of moral action.

Only the observance of the Law (as it were) for its own sake, or rather from the love of God, which is to say the pursuit of justice for its own sake, can fulfill the actual mitzvot and only such pursuit can confer the full benefits of justice. Pursuit of justice for the sake of its benefits leaves open the notorious breach of all systems of law founded on convenience—the breach between expediency and right in cases where benefit and duty do not seem to coincide. Action in the path of the pure pursuit of perfection is built on the recognition that the two as properly gauged cannot fail to coincide.

This I take to be the intension of 'Justice, justice shalt thou pursue!' (*Deuteronomy* 16:20)—that when the path of of justice alone and for its own sake seems to diverge from that of justice as a pragmatic goal (justice for the sake of its benefits) it is justice for its own sake, justice alone we must pursue—intrinsic justice, expressed by the idiom of repetition, rather than instrumental justice. Thus we are commanded to pursue justice when it coincides with apparent self-interest; and, when apparent self-interest diverges from justice, justice again. It is in this sense that I read the requirement, associated with the admonition to adhere to the mitzvot, that the love of God be absolute.

But the introduction of the metaphor of love to begin with can only express the attraction of the aspiring, conscious being towards that which is perfect, divine. The question, then, how love can be commanded does not arise. For this commandment, like the rest, is the natural response of an aspiring being toward that which is Perfection. Nor is there a difficulty in regard to how love can command. For it is notorious that the will of the beloved is at the command of what it conceives to be the will of the lover, without discontinuity or disharmony between the two. The beloved pursues what the lover commands not by logical entailment, nor by coercive compulsion, but by identity of will, value and purpose, hence without heteronomy.

Kant was convinced that the will is the essence of the personality and made the autonomy of the will the sole source of morality. But the will cannot legislate simply its own freedom. This is a contentless concept, a mere formalism as the existentialist moralists have learned by following the logic of Kant's position to its extreme. Epicurus believed autonomy is achieved only by single-minded adherence to the dictate of pleasure, which Kant, following the Stoic critique of hedonistic ethics, found to be the diametrical opposite, the epitome of enslavement. I would prefer to think more dynamically of the personality, in Spinozistic terms: the essence of a being is its tendency or striving (conatus) to preserve, promote, perfect its own being. In conscious beings this conatus is inseparable from that (conscious) aspiration toward perfection which is the recipient ground in which alone the Divine invokes a moral imperative. It is this tendency which hedonists readily confuse with the impetus toward pleasure (by confusing pleasure with its object, our objective wellbeing), and it is this tendency which Kant identified too readily with a faculty of which he believed one could have no knowledge and whose nature, accordingly, he could not specify, the will. If human aspiration toward perfection is, as Spinoza argued, the very identity of the individual (in view of the fact that the essence of all things is their dynamic tendency to preserve and promote—perfect—their own being), then it is clear that there is no heteronomy in allegiance to the obligations laid down by Divinity, properly conceived.

To sum up then, the three questions with which we began are answered: There is no transition from neutral fact to value, for divine existence as conceived monotheistically, is not a neutral fact but a value-laden fact. Still there is no implication from that fact of laws. Rather laws are the imperatives imposed upon, or better called forth within, the minds of aspiring beings by the conception of absolute perfection. These imperatives are specified in human terms by human means to the best of our ability. The process is not difficult since the origins from which the concept of divinity itself arises ultimately are themselves the highest notions of human morality. Moral adequacy is the sole test of the authenticity of any alleged imperative claiming divine authority. As for heteronomy, the application of that notion with regard to the nexus of morality and the monotheistic concept of God is specious. For the locus of the general imperative towards perfection which is the universal content of the divine imperative is the human psyche itself, specifically that aspiring aspect of the moral personality which has at times, simplistically been called the will or even been confused with one small dimension of itself, the appetite for gain or pleasure, but which forms in fact the core identity of the moral person. The divine imperative, then, takes hold from within and is, therefore, a true moral law involving no heteronomy.

But is the moral law entirely unproblematic and so suitable to be used as a touchstone of alleged divine imperatives? In examining this question, I wish to look at three major issues: (1) The basis and the adequacy of the idea of a universal law of life, (2) The question of how far the universal moral principle may be specified, whether to the point of specificity (general rules) and whether to the point of particularity (concrete principles), (3) What bearing diverse circumstances may have, whether natural, social or cultural/traditional, and to what extent imperatives may become over-specified or over-particularized.

(1) The basis of the concept of a universal moral law is the God concept of monotheism itself. If religion is the celebration of the sacred (or of what is held sacred) as such, then monotheism is that form of religion which regards the sacred as unique. The values for which diverse

gods had been devised are now united, and it becomes dialectically inevitable by the working out in history and custom of the logic of the concept of God itself that the projection onto human life of the values now conceived by reference to that single absolute source of value be themselves now conceived as forming a single integrated system, if not in fact then certainly normatively. This is to say it is an ideal of the law as conceived of monotheistically that the principles of law form a single comprehensive system.

The Biblical term for Law, *torah,* denotes a norm conceived as a projection of value upon life. Projection is the etymological connotation, norm is the denotation. The repeated admonition of the Torah "One law shall there be for ye . . .", *i.e.,* that the principle governing a given class of human activities or relations shall be uniform, is the expression of the normative demand that human norms be made systematic (uniform, coherent) as a result of the impact of the monotheistic God concept.[15] It is easy to follow the evolution of the demand for uniformity from historical experience to ethical demand and thence to theological conception and constitutional command. Israelites are told repeatedly that before the law, both formally and in regard to morals, strangers shall be treated and regarded no differently than Israelites: "When a stranger sojourneth with you in your land, you shall not discriminate against him [*lo tonu oto,* the verb is interpreted rabbinically as denoting not only persecution and injustice but invidious speech and attitudes which may be offensive], but the stranger who sojourneth with you shall be as one of your own homeborn citizens. Thou shalt love him as thyself, for ye were strangers in the land of Egypt. I am the Lord your God."[16]

As Hertz remarks: "The duty of loving the stranger is stressed thirty-six times in Scripture and is placed on the same level as kindness to, and protection of, the widow or the orphan." Hermann Cohen correctly detected the reason for this stress, in a passage Hertz cites: "The alien was to be protected, although he was not a member of one's family, clan, religious community or people; simply *because he was a human being.* In the alien, therefore, man discovered the idea of humanity." (See Hertz ap. *Leviticus* 19:33). We begin from the experience of oppression. Thence, to demand for surcease, rest, the opportunity to celebrate the ancestral God, thence to legislation which incorporates norms of equity and charity, thence to the conception of a universal God, universal source of nature's being and its order, universal standpoint of the universal truth, who projects values universally and from whose universality is reflected the universal norm of reciprocity, mutuality, inter-subjectivity, out of the psychological foundation laid by historic experience. We were strangers, so we must treat strangers kindly. This inference does not follow by the laws of logic but only via those of psychology, which identifies by association with others in like positions to those in which one conceives himself. But the principle is given as a rule, a law of constitutional scope, not an affection of sentiment. How is the transformation achieved from an emotional tendency (which might equally be countered by other sentiments such as those of alienness or fear or demands for vengeance) to a categorical moral demand? Only by reference to the Absolute Standard of value, before whom all human individuals are alike. Hence the closing line: "I am the Lord your God." 'You were strangers . . .' gives the sentimental motive, but 'I am the Lord thy God' gives the reason.

In a tribal society or primitive civilization where right is proportioned to power[17] it might seem absurd to claim that the standing of the orphan, widow or stranger before law is and ought to be no less than that of the most powerful and prosperous citizen. From the standpoint of an absolute source of all values, their standing can be no less. Thus it is the monotheistic concept of God which renders possible the universalization of the principle of mutuality not only to the helpless or potentially disadvantaged or oppressed but to all persons as a categorical command that they love one another as they love themselves. And this universalization, which creates the cardinal moral principle, is achieved without the aid of syllogisms or induction (as though syllogisms or induction could compass the universalization of a *moral* principle!) solely through the reflection of what begins as sentiment or affection, against the concept of a universal divinity. For it is only in the light of Objectivity (which is itself a norm projected onto history and science as well as human relations from the monotheistic concept of Divinity) that we can regard our fellows' subjecthood (and hence their deserts) as the moral equivalent of our own. [8]

What claim is made by reciprocity, mutuality, the regarding of one's fellow as one's moral equal? From a Christian point of view it might seem a call to self-sacrifice is involved. There is a tendency to read 'Love thy fellow as thyself' in reference to 'Greater love hath no man than this, that he lay down his life for his friends.' But there is no basis for such a reading in the Hebrew texts or in the logic of the concepts they invoke. The oriental idea of self-sacrifice is not enunciated here as a value norm. Nor are conditions contemplated in which the loss of one person would be preferable to that of another. On the contrary, from the standpoint of Objectivity there is no net gain if one person's interests are sacrificed for the sake of another's. *A fortiori,* not if the interest in question is life. Only such mythic notions as arbitrary election to grace and vicarious atonement in an arbitrary retributive scheme can bring such a value into the sphere of ethics, (just as it is the romantic appeal to sentiment which brings it into poetry) and then only in extraordinary circumstances. In ordinary circumstances the notion that the sacrifice of a life might even be appropriate, regardless whether it were deemed desirable, would be simply incorrect. The rule of mutuality, however, the principle of equal regard for others' subjecthood alongside one's own, is not presented with a view to such rarefied contexts but as the general rule of human living. Its principle is that one should not demand as a right for oneself what one does not regard as a right for others, and that one should accord as a right to others whatever one expects as a right for oneself.

The command of reciprocity is a command against moral solipsism. To say of this command that it does not imply a duty of self-sacrifice for the sake of another is not to say that it can make no demands of positive action (regardless of cost) for the sake of the good of others or particularly for the sake of the common good or the public or general good. It has long been a dogma of specious liberalism that liberality is voluntary and thus cannot be commanded. The claim is to be predicated, insofar as it might be argued, on the fact that I cannot be obliged to sacrifice myself for others' interests by the rule of reciprocity since that rule cannot impart greater objective import to their interests than to mine. But this argument is limited in scope. It suggests the exaggerated and dramatic type of case in which I am called upon to sacrifice large interests of mine (or all my interests, life itself) to small or disproportionate interests of another. It cannot prove that there is no case in which it would be an obligation for me to sacrifice some interest of mine in behalf of an interest—say a larger or more pressing interest—of another. Yet classic liberals have tended to assume that there can never be such a case.

In fact, historically, the argument has been that I give preference to my own interests over those of others by a law of nature and that it is foolhardy to attempt to countermand a law of nature ethically. This was the reasoning of the classic liberals and ultimately of their forebears the Sophists, who made much hay with sayisms to the effect that egoism is the law of nature. To begin with, the natural "facts" upon which such remarks are based (and on which in turn may be founded both smug self-satisfaction and indignant exposés) are only part of the story. There are many natural laws, not one, and other-supporting actions and behaviors are widespread not only among humans but among numerous species of mammals, birds, and insects, as sociobiologists in recent years have demonstrated quite extensively. Edward Wilson's *Sociobiology*[19] offers extensive illustration of behavior which Wilson terms altruistic. This choice of word may be unfortunate in that it suggests motives of an anthropomorphic sort, or, alternatively in that it tends to promote a drift toward reduction of human altruism to a genetically endowed mechanism, vitiating its ethical significance, but there are at any rate numerous well attested behaviors of sharing, helping, cooperating, and indeed self-sacrifice by individuals in the animal kingdom, and there are (pace the followers of Spencer) good evolutionary models for the biological utility (adaptiveness) of such behaviors in a population.

Secondly, and at least as importantly, the dubious naturalism upon which classical liberalism is founded affords no basis for ethical conclusions. Granted that selfishness is *a* law of nature, ethics may demand more of us than nature does—at least more than nature does when nature is considered from the perspective of selfishness as a lowest common denominator among natural acts. The Sophist suasion 'What can one expect?' is for this reason indeed a sophism—It equivocates on 'expectation,' as though our moral expectations were necessarily to be tailored to our most disappointing empirical experience or our most pessimistic estimates of potential performance. This may be a useful practical stratagem in many social contexts (*i.e.,* if our objective is to minimize disappointment), but it is not for that reason an appropriate description of all human behavior, still less a sound foundation for an allegedly ethical principle.

The illusion that reciprocity extends only to the matter of mutual non-interference, toleration, however, is a fulcrum for the isolation of negative from positive liberty, the spurious notion that freedom can consist solely in the absence of active external hindrance, to the exclusion of any provision for material welfare. Stated thus baldly, the proposition is plainly absurd. The two sorts of freedom are patently interdependent. But classical liberals tend to assume that since (by the law of nature) I cannot be required to give up anything of mine in your behalf, I have fulfilled my obligations to you if I do not actively interfere with you. Hence the desire to give precedence to negative liberty over positive liberty and even in some quarters to eliminate the latter in favor of the former.

But the Biblical command is not a negative rule of reciprocity, informing me only that I may harm no one, but rather a positive rule involving the positive recognition of others' subjecthood. By this is meant a positive obligation to assist (as in the laws of gleaning and paradigmatically in the command to aid with a fallen beast). I am to love my fellow as myself, not merely to avoid harming him, but to go out of my way to assist him, not as a matter of charity which I am free to withhold but as a matter of obligation. Further the principle of marginal utility is relaxed to the extent that the subjects of the Law may exact no interest on loans or even retain a daily worker's hire overnight. These principles violate the archcanon of that tightfisted liberalism which maintains that without an explicit contractual agreement I can have no positive obligations to another, which is to say the dogma that I can bear no positive obligations to another which I do not recognize to be in my interest. How is this principle derived which contravenes that specious liberalism which holds liberality to be a matter of conscience and then (often) goes on to dismiss conscience as the soft headedness of small spirits?

Of course, it would be possible to derive *similar* provisions from the prudential counsel that one might one day find oneself in need of un-promised help. But this prudential rule would not be the equivalent of the moral rule in question. For charity (etc.) on this account would be mere insurance and so confer a benefit in the form of protection against risk. And in that case there would always be the option for the "hard-headed" to opt for self-insurance. There would be no question of an unconditioned obligation to aid others; but that is what the Biblical rule entails. Thus again the reference to God: The obligation is categorical, not conditioned on my perception of my potential needs.

As with most of the central moral principles embedded in the Law, the positive rather than merely restrictive application of the Biblical principle of reciprocity was well understood by the Sages and articulated by them conceptually as a distinctive juridical rule: '*kofin 'al middat Sedom*'— "We enforce against the ethos of Sodom."[20] This might sound rather lurid in the context of contemporary associations of Sodom with deviant sexual practices, but the principle is understood quite otherwise by its rabbinic promulgators. The ethos of Sodom, that is the customary and habitual (and therefore conceptually formulable) mode of behavior (and thus disposition of character) properly associated with Sodom in accordance with the Biblical story of Lot is inhospitality. The Sodomites did not recognize the rights of guests. That they may have entertained loathesome intentions toward the strangers Lot had taken under the shelter of his roof only shows the extremity which they had reached in their failure to accord the welcome due to strangers or to recognize the obligations the guest relationship entailed. The stranger (*ger*) was not a mere alien (compare the Greek *xenos*) but a guest, client, friend, whose interests the patron/host felt required to protect with the same zeal as those of a family member—or greater in the heat of Lot's moral em-barrassment at the violation by his neighbors of his attempt at bestowal of sanctuary. The welcome Lot had offered was the strangers' due, their right, if the word is not out of place, which he could not rightfully withhold or take back again once tendered.

The vice (*middah* pejoratively construed) of the Sodomites was their customary and habitual refusal of hospitality, based on the attitude cited at Mishnah *Avot* (5:10) "Mine is mine; thine is thine." What, we might wonder is so wrong with that? It is not rapacity that is in question, but simply privacy—or so it might appear.

To the liberal sensibility it seems evident that in a system of plural rational interests the interests of all are maximized by the principle of *suum cuique,* each looking to his own and not interfering with his fellow, neither abetting nor hindering except with regard to what is due—*e.g.* aiding by means mutually, contractually agreed to be beneficial, hindering, with due process of law where a penalty civil or criminal is needed to right some imbalance which has occurred or forestall some damage to the whole system of equilibria of interests. Liberals from the times of Epicurus and Lucretius have presumed that the best social policy is that of laissez faire, that an attitude of detached amusement[21] is the most socially beneficial one to take toward the plight of our fellow humans— far superior to the meddlesome desire to improve their lot and lives, which soon transforms itself into a wish to improve *them* and so to impose ourselves and our ways upon them.

But this presumes too much. It presumes, to be precise, that we cannot aid without imposing, a presumption which the Torah challenges with its articulation of the moral command as being that we should love our fellows as we love ourselves—as they love themselves and as we would wish ourselves to be loved, plainly not meddlesomely but with what we ourselves would recognize as aid if we were they. Classic liberalism presumes moreover, highly dubiously, that the most generous activity we can engage in is *"cultiver notre jardin,"* and that the maximization of global social utility is to be derived from the universalization of an attitude of benign neglect. This seems, if experience is any teacher, plainly to be false. The same invisible hand which fails to guide economies toward the maximization of their potentials without guidance and restraint of the individuals and corporations at work in them plainly will exercise no mysterious providence over the general quality of life merely because individuals mind their own business. On the contrary, I lose if my neighbor will not lend me his power saw, and the loss is compounded when I in turn refuse him the use of my power drill. Society at large loses from the universalization of an ethos of impersonality, coldness, formality, universal alienation and anomie, husbands and wives signing contracts and treaties with one another, and the like.

Far from a maximization of benefits, the universalization of strict property notions (applied even to the human body and the most intimate human relations, as though to prevent the dissolution of barriers between and among human beings—even between husband and wife) seems rather to lead to a no-win game. This I think was the intent of Rabbi Yohanan's remark that "Jerusalem was destroyed because its denizens judged within it according to the Torah." "What then, the Sages asked, should they have followed the Law of the Magians? The point was that they judged strictly on the basis of the Law and did not expand beyond the strict legal sentence."[22] What Rabbi Yohanan observed was that the

Torah as a law of life is predicated on the assumption that there will be concession, compromise, generosity, and that its system will not function without these. Strict insistence on the sentence of the law creates only legalism, not justice. Liberalism, presuming the natural equation of rationality with rapacity and the ultimacy of material/hedonic goods, seeks only to regulate the pursuit of these goods in an orderly civil system. The Torah presumes the possibility of generosity and the recognition that it may be rational to give, indeed that there are goods to gain beyond material goods (peace, love, and justice being among them) which it would be rational to seek even at great material cost. The question of which view of human nature might be more "realistic" is of little moment if the Biblical/Talmudic sensibility is correct in its prophetic assessment that no society can stand except upon the basis of an ethos in accordance with the latter (perhaps somewhat ideal) view of man. The prophetic warning or insight is grounded in an awareness that the life of a society depends on more than law. It depends on give and take. And, in view of what we know of the general inefficiency of all mechanisms and the even greater inefficiency of human social mechanisms relative to the rest, it should not seem surprising that the Torah prescribes rather more give than take.

The Biblical rule applies by reference to the concept of recognition of others' subjecthood, demanding (and this is *sui generis* a demand of morals, not merely of prudence) that one regard the other's position as though one were in it oneself and not only feel but respond according to the judgment of interests one would make in one's own case, applying one's actual powers to the other who is fictively taken in place of oneself. The subjective transference this requires from one's own position to that of one's fellow rests upon reference to the divine standpoint, which regards all subjecthoods (*ceteris paribus*) as morally equal. This is not the "natural" (*i.e.,* sophistic) stance, which aids the pretensions of the moral superiority of the first person and facilitates that moral myopia which holds the world to recede perspectivally from oneself in all directions to a set of infinitesimal moral vanishing points. Rather, it is the belief in the objective equal desert of all, applied not as a piece of rhetoric but as a practical rule. Assisting the conception behind this crucial moral move toward the recognition of others' subjecthood is the concept of a special or unique relation between every subject and the Absolute, a relationship symbolized by the metaphor of divine regard and favor (*ḥesed*), which reflects back into the positive concept which gives content to the reciprocity rule, the concept of human kindness (*ḥesed*) and love. The foundation, then, of the command of human reciprocal love is the reciprocal love of God and man, by which is meant the concept of divine aid of humans universally and the command of human love for God, that is human regard of the divine perfection, which is the motive of the human aspiration toward perfection and so the linchpin of the Law.[23]

(2) The Biblical command, then, is not a merely formal principle of mutuality. It is a material principle of love. This fact is crucial, for it is all that distinguishes the Biblical command from an emptiness to be filled in ad libitum by whatever notion one might possibly regard as relevant, as was done, to take an egregious but factual example, by Sade, who promised that he would treat his victims in no manner in which he would not find it perfectly acceptable for others to treat him. The love which is commanded toward fellow persons is not defined subjectively but only measured by reference to the notion of subjecthood. It is defined by reference to God, that is through the aspiration of all self-conscious subjects toward divine perfection. It is this fact which makes its content objectively specifiable, as an obligation to help rather than to hinder, regardless of the empiric inclination one may bear towards oneself (which may be warped or twisted) and regardless of the empiric concession some may make regarding "self-insurance." They may say: 'This is a risk I am willing to take for myself,' but that in no way legitimates an insistence that others bear the same risk. In fact it does not even legitimate their taking it. For desires are not self-legitimating, and the command of self-love is implicitly presupposed in the command to love others. I must assist others towards what is perfection for them regardless of my willingness to forego their assistance of me. Indeed, I am obliged *not* to forego their assistance, insofar as I require it, and insofar as it *is* assistance.

How far can the requirements of the love of others be specified? Plainly they do not countenance unprovoked aggression. Plainly they require assistance. But in the definition of what constitutes assistance, the best standard generally (although not always) is the self-perceived self-project of those others themselves, provided that this project is conceived maturely (realistically) and moderated by a due regard for the objective needs of others. This is the true form of liberalism, founded on the recognition that others can be (and should be) the best judges of their own interest and firmly rooted in the language of the Biblical command to love our fellows as we love ourselves, which is to say to love them with the same love with which they love themselves, a love we know first-hand from the rational conception at its best of the love with which we love ourselves.

In answer to our second question, then, the divine law specifies a rule of reciprocity, not the looking on ourselves or others with that divine detachment which is so evident in the operation of nature, for this impersonality, as is notorious, is beyond the scope of human moral comprehension, but rather the application in the social/moral sphere of the highest ethical principle we know, which is the principle defined by reference to the concept of a God of absolute perfection, that we should regard and treat our fellows with the same concern with which we at our most rational (perfection oriented) regard and act in behalf of ourselves, viewing them as subjects whose self-conceived perception of their own interests, while not inviolable, is sacred and to be treated with the same respect that we at our most rational might hope for toward ourselves.

(3) There is a great watershed in ethics between (a.) the tradition which maintains with Plato that it is never possible on the basis of mere human knowledge to formulate a universal moral rule which will legitimately apply to all the situations it purports to govern and (b.) the Biblical tradition, which has become the backbone of the Judaeo-Christian ethical tradition and of the philosophical ethics of Kant, which maintains that the specification of such rules to the level of relating to concrete, describable actions is possible. By the Platonic position I do not mean of course the sophistical claim that value is the object of any interest or wholly relative to the subjective impressions or actual needs of the moral agent or beholder. Nor do I mean the popular position which has been dignified by the title situation ethics. For this can mean no more than that there is no objective right except as determined by the perceptions of participants. But I mean a rather strict situationism, which holds that there is an objectively right course in any situation but that it cannot be specified by any general rule.

Plato argues for this claim by the use of examples intended to show that given certain information regarding a situation, it is always possible to reverse the tenor of what might be assumed the correct moral stance or judgment by the addition of further data, hitherto concealed. Since human knowledge is finite, it follows that no universal rule concrete enough to specify the type of action it prescribes or proscribes (such as rules against murder, theft or lying) can be taken with assurance to be right in every case to which it is held to apply. This does not mean, of course, that Plato holds laws to be impossible or human moral judgment to be unattainable. On the contrary, he believes both laws and moral judgment to be necessary requisites of human life as such. But for Plato all human laws and judgments are only very rough approximations of the truth, which must in the best circumstances be estimated afresh in every case by a mature and seasoned judgment, which even so will all too often be found wanting. Paradigmatically for Plato, I cannot condemn the murder of infants categorically, for there may be reasons of state or force majeure (not to mention the familiar case of deformity) which justify the taking of even such a step. Or, to choose what Plato would regard as quite an unproblematic illustration, I cannot condemn categorically the slaying of all infants, for if I had the knowledge that my practice would not be imitated or otherwise adversely affect crucial social structures and if I knew that by the slaying of this infant I was nipping in the bud the career of some Hitler, then reason, by the Platonic account would not only urge but command me to take the step.

With this the monotheistic tradition takes the strongest issue. What makes possible the enunciation of an alternative is not some superior source of knowledge of the unseen events of the future and the unseen intents of others' minds which assures monotheists that their moral choices if kept concordant with certain rules will be invariably for the best. For there is no such knowledge. Rather it is a set of moral presumptions (that is fictions based on fact), in this case paradigmatically the presumed innocence of all human beings until they prove guilty by their own acts.

For the Christian, the doctrine of original sin renders the global presumption of innocence globally false. But still it forms the basis of Christian ethics (Judge not . . .), and on this foundation we can still speak of a Judaeo-Christian ethical tradition. For the Jew, innocence can be a fact. But we know empirically, statistically that for the world it might be better if a certain proportion of infants were not to be born. We are fond of saying that we are not gods to judge which they are in advance. But is not inconceivable that with advances in behavioral science beyond its present muling and puking infancy, we might someday form an educated guess of just which babes to watch. Even with our present very spotty knowledge of behavioral genetics, proposals have not been wanting which suggest we do just that. And it is not incomprehensible that in some future state of knowledge we might be able to pinpoint with a fair degree of accuracy just which infants it is best should never be raised. Plato's science was by far inferior to ours but even he believed that with regard to certain classes he could make a fairly educated guess, and if he had our knowledge or that which our descendents will have he would hardly hesitate to modify and in specific areas to expand his "little list." But this precisely is what monotheistic law forbids, and that quite regardless of the presumptive social costs.

We believe in free will, an axiom whose supposition is implicitly supposed in any formulation of an imperative or command, as Kant pointed out emphatically and Maimonides long before him.[24] Despite the seeming preponderance of evidence and the weight of causal influences, we presume that moral choice is possible: "All is determined, but choice is granted." And on the basis of this supposition, a moral postulate whether or not it is a law of nature, we can tip the scales of judgment towards a presumption of innocence (*lechaf zechût*), even overbalancing the weight of evidence, on the basis of a hope which we may not regard as probable of realization—not only can but must so tip the scales. This is the entire basis of our system of justice. We can and must assume that it is better, *i.e.,* more just morally, not materially, not more pragmatically useful in every case (Heaven knows!) to exonerate the guilty than to inculpate the innocent. With the aid of this presumption we can temper justice with mercy and so formulate laws in spite of human error's inevitability, because our rule will be when erring to try to err on the side of mercy, and because we know that when we err in that fashion, the error is not absolute, but quite likely in many ways a blessing in itself, since the exoneration of the guilty can be (through the strange dynamics of the human psyche) as strong a force in their possible regeneration as their inculpation is hoped to be, and at times it can be stronger.

The conceptual foundation for the presumption of innocence and the judgment of others generally in a scale tipped to some degree (and in some respects to an absolute degree—for this we call privacy) in their favor rests squarely on the Biblical command of reciprocity. For that is just how we might wish to be judged ourselves. Each human being here is viewed from the perspective of his own subjecthood; and, the transference from our subjectivity to his is accomplished by reference to the divine objectivity (hence no favoring of persons or of the stations of the rich or poor), not with the mythic eye of God which knows the moral future, the prescience which is ascribed to those desirous of "playing God" in cases of euthanasia and the like, but with the simple eye of objectivity which enables us to regard others as human subjects in their own right rather than merely furniture in our own moral world. This intersubjective perspective, is made possible through monotheism precisely because without monotheism there is no ground for departure from moral solipsism, no basis for the conception of a reality outside the mind.[25] It can be formulated without monotheistic presuppositions, but only as a pure fiction in that case. To regard the subjecthood of others as real and so of equal moral weight to our own we must assume that the divine objectivity is real as well, and that is what makes possible for us the formulation of moral rules and laws which reach the level of the concrete and particular.

The specification of moral obligations has both a quantitative and a qualitative dimension. Quantitatively, I think it would be an error to attempt to specify the extent of human obligations. They are both too ramified and too varied with circumstances to be capable of quantitative formulation. Kant's distinction between perfect and imperfect obligations is perhaps the closest substitute for a quantitative account of obligation, and this amounts merely to a recognition that there are some obligations which rightfully cannot be neglected and manifold others among which we must choose. But there is one quantitative matter which

I feel is capable of clarification and more than a little in need of it, the matter of the allocation of our energies and resources between ourselves and others.

Plainly the equal positive worth ascribed to human deserts requires, in the abstract, that my obligations to others be no less than my obligation to myself. This might seem to imply a moral obligation on my part toward others which far exceeds—indeed eclipses my obligation to myself since others far outnumber me. But the reasoning would be spurious, as is obvious when it is considered that the assumption of the equal worth of all cannot lead to the elimination of my obligation to myself. The speciousness of the reasoning lies in the neglect of the aliquot shares of others' responsibility toward themselves, toward me and toward each other. I cannot be held morally obligated by the failure of others to do their share, although I would be obliged to aid in establishing a system which tends to ensure, to the extent possible and reasonable, that they, as well as I, do our shares.

It would be foolish, to be sure, to attempt to set an upper limit to the extent of my obligations to others beyond saying that morally I ought not to assume a self-destructive burden..It seems unfair as well as counter-productive to alienate from anyone more than half the product (or profit) of his energies in work. That seems to follow from the reasoning in the paragraph above, and seems, in effect, to define the limits of slavery, at least insofar as the significance of such an institution can be expressed in quasi-quantitative terms. But there are contexts, particularly in the family and in certain kinds of voluntarily undertaken endeavor—humanitarian, military, spiritual, educational—or even in activities of a rather mundane seeming service nature, where an individual will expend far more than half of what energies or resources he has to expend without appearing to have wronged himself. The reason is that such actions are undertaken out of love, friendship or kindred motivating emotions based on identification of one's own interests with those of one's beneficiary. Crucial to the moral rightness of such actions is their voluntariness, the sense in the agent not only of freedom in assuming a commitment but of self-fulfillment rather than self-curtailment through its sustained execution.

With regard to the more impersonal mode of obligation towards others, one's fellow citizens and fellow human beings at large, one's material obligations, that is, the responsibilities one is obliged to assume in behalf of others whether or not one finds those obligations fulfilling or rewarding, the moral wrongness of slavery requires that they be set at well below half of one's total expenditure of human energies—not more than half because that would constitute slavery, but less than half, so as to maintain the freedom of an individual to establish primary commitments to family, close colleagues, friends or particular ideals of his own choice in view of his primary bonds of affiliation and identification.

It is neither arbitrary nor unfair that such bonds be established, and their justification need not be founded on such homely (and sometimes self-serving) maxims as "charity begins at home"—another appeal to Sophistic naturalism (that is, egoism). Rather their utility and moral warrant follow from the general inefficiency of all organized systems, not least, of all human social systems. If I am to expend energies in behalf of others, there must be some social system through which their distribution is allocated. The closer, the more intimate, the more reciprocal the bonds (and the feedback loops) within that system, the more appropriately is it possible for my energies to be expended. It is for this reason—or, rather, because human beings are capable of recognizing this truth—that no social system has been capable of dislodging the family as the prime focal point of human energy. And, morally speaking (despite the aesthetic appeal of logically simpler utopian schematisms), it is evident that none ought to have that capability.

There is no legitimacy to the notion that one ought to love the world at large with the same kind of love one attaches to one's spouse or children, closest friends or comrades. Even fellow countrymen and one's own people are subject to a special kind of love in virtue of the bonds of reciprocity by which the dispersion of energies in their behalf is prevented from being merely diffuse, although one may have an obligation to work for that ideal state in which humanity at large recognize toward one another bonds of reciprocity similar to those which hold among the members of a well integrated people or nation. I am required to love others as myself in the sense of promoting their striving for perfection, not in the sense of attaching to them the same intimacy and personal regard I discover in my relations with family members or even close associates or fellow citizens.

Taking into account the self-appropriated values in behalf of which human energies are expended including those expended in behalf of one's own family, close friends, high ideals (including those not thought of often in romantic terms, the simple virtues of ordinary life, fidelity, thoroughness, truthfulness, hard work, small scale kindness and consideration as well as the lofty sights of Service to Mankind), it would appear that not *less* than half one's energies should be expended in behalf of others. Indeed, there are conditions in which duty toward one's self-appropriated values and ideals might well call forth a total giving or even sacrifice. By contrast, liberty requires that in behalf of impersonal, non-appropriable, non-appropriated or alienated duties, not *more* than half, indeed much less than half one's energies would rightfully be demanded.

The modulation of the equilibrium between self, "extended self" (*i.e.,* others conceived in relation to one's self-concept) and others (*i.e.,* others conceived impersonally) is the central issue of interpersonal politics. The crucial issue of liberal as opposed to totalitarian systems of government is that the former preserve while the latter disrespect the right (and need) of the individual to form his own self-concept, *i.e.,* to seek perfection by way of the means he alone is best capable of discovering, conceiving, appropriating and fulfilling.

A critical corollary of the foregoing reasoning is that when human energies are expressed in monetary terms (as many of them often are in a money economy, where money becomes a medium of exchange of energies, it is wrong of the state (which is the rightful guardian of the impersonal other) to lay claim to more than half or even close to half the wage-earned income of any individual in ordinary circumstances, for that is to preempt the major share of that person's product, in essence to enslave him—or to enslave him by shares, to put the matter more precisely.

This argument holds true only for wage-earned income of course. With unearned income, beyond the limits necessary to life, a considerably larger share for public use might be demanded or expected. Vast accumulations of wealth should be shared or they lose all moral claim to legitimacy. Proceeds and profits of enterprise too should be shared, both in behalf of appropriated ideals and in behalf of impersonal public goals. But for the impersonal concerns, half might be a fair stopping point for strict requirement, with proper incentives for the allocation of further resources toward individually appropriated conceptions of the common good. In this way the state and (say) the private firm/foundation would be yoked as partners in a common enterprise (which still preserved the liberty of a plural choice of values and visions in behalf of which resources might be expended) rather than their participants' being encouraged to view themselves as mutual enemies engaged in a process of mutual despoliation.

It may seem that public need might be so great as to require more than half the total available energies of a population or of some class within a population. The first case would describe a dire public emergency, the second an inequity, which would require in time to be rectified. Given a moderately equitable social scheme and conditions of relative tranquillity (no immediate threat of insurmountable public disaster), only unconscionable social inefficiency (*e.g.,* a rapacious and pervasive bureaucracy) would require so high an expenditure of the individual, amounting to a kind of oppression—enslavement or exploitation. In ordinary circumstances, if most people do their share, less than half should be more than ample for all obligatory public needs. If this is so, human effort will produce a tremendous surplus to be expended freely in self-perfection and that mode of self-expression which aims at aiding in the self-perfection of others.

The closer integration of a society and the widening of value perspectives to make possible the self-appropriation of a wider sphere of other-regarding activity make possible a kind of affluence of human energies and thereby enhance the freedom of self-expression in this area, making possible a wider choice of avenues of self-fulfillment and encouraging the commitment of larger shares of human energies to the more freely chosen and more closely appropriated projects than would otherwise have occurred.

It is easy to imagine numerous improvements to the human condition materially, morally and intellectually, were enlarged loyalties and more widely conceived bonds of attachment to be adopted widely, and that makes the moral principle we are enunciating sound somewhat utopian. But it differs from the maxims of properly utopian schemes in that (*pace* the Sophists) it does not rest upon the predication of a change in human nature. For if the key to voluntary appropriation of a higher proportion of other regarding goals and a widening of their sphere of application is a widening of the sphere of personal identification (diminution of the sense of alienation), then it seems clear that there are mechanisms built upon the natural desires of human beings to grow and share in common profit and mutual recognition which will assure the widening of human moral perspectives.

Profit sharing schemes are a model of such mechanisms. So in another way are schemes of granting honor and respect. The same models and others like them can be expanded and applied far more widely. If it is imprudent to deprive the firm of more than half its profits, lest its managers come to see their efforts as a frustrating struggle for another's gain, so also it is imprudent to expect workers' productivity to be spurred by abstract notions of selfless (or long distance) goals to be gained. As a general social rule, the surest way to ensure that each individual does his share (or more) is to ensure, as on the old whaling ships, that each individual has a stake materially, morally, intellectually, and spiritually in the outcome of his efforts. Human generosity will follow naturally when there are the liberty and the resources to allow it. It will be naturally made more handsome when encouraged by appropriate social institutions and widely exampled for emulation.

As for the question of the degree of qualitative specification possible in imperatives, I think it is clear that in principle they must be specifiable to the level of particularity (as in the conclusions of Aristotle's practical syllogisms) if they are to be regarded as the directive principles of particular actions. But it is also plain that statements of rules, by virtue of their universal form (except in certain special contexts with certain specially designed formulations) cannot be regarded as operating at the level of particularity. Moreover, the most universal norm, that of the pursuit of perfection, reaches the level of particularity in so many and so diverse ways that it would lose its normative force altogether were it not possible to regard many of these as representing alternate modes of fulfillment open to beings of finite capability. But this implies that no one particular mode of perfection, taken in abstraction from the general imperatives without which perfection is impossible, can be regarded as imperative to the extent that its achievement is more or less precluded by the pursuit of others. Here we confront the legitimate realm of that freedom which is based solely on taste, style and preference, for there can be no rational determinants of choice among alternative avenues toward objective perfection in the case where each of those avenues is as valuable intrinsically, as valid instrumentally and as accessible as the rest.

Again, while moral principles drawn from the counsel of perfection must reach the level of particularity yet are in the foregoing respect necessarily under-specified, in another sense they may be over-specified, and this occurs by virtue of their involvement in the symbolic realm and is the foundation of ritual. Adequate expression of vital and essential relationships (man/God, man/man, man/woman, man/nature, etc.) is among the counsels of perfection. But the language of such expression is symbol, and the logic of symbol is not that of the logicians but that of expressive association. The modes of symbolic associative response are both conventional (as predominant in language) and natural (as predominant in music) as well as combined (in both language and music and, say, in song)—contextual, cultural. For this reason the requirements of ritual may be specified far beyond the level that moral imperatives alone can specify—not beyond the level of particularity, of course, but into artifactually created symbolic ranges of particularity each with a cultural significance within the context of a given social framework or system of frameworks or within the context of world culture. Through the expressive extension of moral significance via symbols there can be moral force even in contextual imperatives whose elements would familiarly be identified as conventional.

Finally there is the interpenetration of the two modes, the under-specification of free self-creation and the overspecification of symbolic expression. This confluence, I think, has more than a little to do with the life of the artist, and I think that it is clear in such a case how the imperative force of the counsels of perfection may be preserved even here, where they may apply to but one individual and that in a context whose elements are not only conventional but also in large measure the product of a single creative intelligence.

Apropos the issue of overspecification, I have been asked whether the treatment I have accorded this matter does not render merely conventional the whole realm of ritual and any dimension of human behavior which relies upon the symbolic/expressive repertoire of ritual, and if merely conventional is this realm not merely arbitrary as well? How in that case is it possible to regard one system of ritual/symbolic specifications as in any way superior to another? How in the Biblical/Talmudic case is it possible to regard the laws and customs of Israel as any closer to the word of God than say those of the head hunters of New Guinea—or, to put the matter, if it can be, still more pointedly, how can they be held to be superior to the more ancient rites, say of the Canaanites or the Egyptians against which they so vigorously militate.

Part of the answer is implicit already in our discussions of the purgation of evil from the concept of divinity and the concomitant drive toward the humanization of human mores. The aesthetic of monotheistic ritual must be one of sweetness, goodness and light for the same reason that the monotheistic ethic cannot be one of violence, darkness and fear. Moreover it is erroneous to suppose that because ritual relies upon elements of convention it is therefore arbitrary. Far too much has been made (not only by the early Protestant theologians but also by many readers of the traditional Jewish texts) of the distinction between moral ordinances and ritual statutes. The moral ordinances themselves depend, for their specification to the level of particularity, upon the introduction of a ritual-like degree of particularization. Thus for example the laws against theft, man-stealing, incest and even rape cannot be specified to a level of behavioral applicability without the elaboration of intricate systems of definitions and conditions to define the acts to which these laws make reference—employing concepts of property, privacy, dignity, etc. which are, so far as behavior is concerned, arbitrarily defined (not in the core, to be sure, but at the fringes). And, as I have endeavored to make plain, even laws which would appear to hold no prima facie moral force may yet *acquire it* within a given social context. To that extent their moral relevance may be very real although their foundation is pure convention.

But in this latter case, the case that is of norms established solely on the basis of convention—*e.g.,* morals may require in a given situation that we apologize but social conventions specify the expressive modalities, qualitatively and quantitatively, by which this is to be done—plainly the moral force of the moral imperative is carried over into the particularistic expressive realm. It becomes a moral obligation to use the recognized social modes in our social intercourse. Hence the broadening of the Sages' dictum *'Dina demalchuta dina'* from its historic meaning: 'The ordinances of the Imperium are law' to its more familiar meaning: 'The law of the realm is the law.'

Still confining ourselves to the level of ritual or ettiquette, if you will (for it is obvious that when morals conflict with common usage morals ought to prevail), there are important exceptions to the principle of adopting the prevalent language of social usage (or, in a pluralistic situation, adopting a kind of lowest common denominator or pidgin constructed from various familiar alternatives). For the symbolic usages of a given culture, as traditions, may become so significant as expressions of cultural continuity through time and across distance, especially through the fact that many have lived by them and died for them, that these symbols in their very particularity become worthy of retention and that to a degree which exceeds the merely general moral force of the values for which they stand.

If it is asked, however, whether the account which I have given makes clear the superiority of one set of purely ritual standards over another—why then I must reply, of course, that it does and it does not. There is aesthetic judgment by means of which the purely or strictly moral canon may be supplemented, and that itself can give a moral force to the extent that the more civilized, tasteful and apt modes of symbolic expression *ceteris paribus* are to be preferred to the less so where there is a choice. But there remains the irreducible fact that one mode of ritual expression cannot be judged inherently, *i.e.*, intrinsically (without contextual references) superior to another solely by virtue of its belonging or not belonging to a given mode or set of symbolic expressions. With reference to the particular institutions of Jewish ritual, for example, what this means is that they may be superior to some alternatives in virtue of the values to which they refer, to others in virtue of the aptness of their stylistic mode, but there is no way in which they can be claimed *a priori* to be superior *per se* to their alternatives. Indeed, I might add, nowhere in the corpus of traditional pronouncements on the role and status of these statutes do we find any categorical claim as to their superiority or their universal applicability to all rational beings—quite the contrary, they are the laws and usages of Israel, an existentially constituted community, and they receive sufficient validation if they function adequately in that regard.

Even so, I wish to emphasize that the element of convention in symbolism does not render one system of symbols morally interchangeable with another, as though the choice among them were only a matter of taste. For the common use of known symbolisms renders them objectively significant in the cultural context they help create. And the preferability of one system over another may become in this regard not merely a matter of tone or style but a moral issue subject to stringent imperatives. More than an inkling of this is contained in the Biblical/Mishnaic inclusion of the prohibition of blasphemy to sons of Noah, that is the Mosaic inclusion of the prohibition of blasphemy not merely to Israelites but to humanity at large. In view of the ease with which this (in our times crucial) point can be misinterpreted, I think it may deserve some elucidation. An excellent paradigmatic illustration is the recently much debated issue of an alleged right to parade the swastika in Skokie, Illinois.

Liberals and would-be liberals find themselves in something of a quandary when faced with the question of whether members of the American Nazi Party (or comparable organizations) should be permitted to parade, demonstrate, make speeches in Nazi regalia, displaying the swastika and other symbols and reminders of the Nazi cult of violence which swept the world into the holocaust of the Second World War, whose memory has already begun to fade, and whose announced policies and avowed passions consummated the destruction of six million Jews and dealt to the people of Israel a blow from which it is not yet clear demographically that we can recover.

In the theory of liberalism only actions can be restrained and then only when they involve actual or potential harm to their victims. There is, of course, a distinction to be drawn between material and mental harm. And, while it is possible for an aggressor by verbal abuse and symbolic intimidation to inflict far more grievous damage mentally in many cases than could readily be compassed physically, the moral as opposed to physical nexus between human beings is thought to be so tenuous and the range of the psychically offensive or noxious so arbitrary that the law tends to look away from the non-physical form of assault in all but the most egregious cases and to place the burden of evidence and (strangely) the presumption of responsibility on the injured or offended party in the remainder—as though it were up to the beholder what sights and symbols would sear or scar the mind.

The realm of thought, of course, is free, and so, by extension, is the realm of expression. The nominalistic metaphysic from which liberalism springs would hold thought of little account which could not be freely articulated in words or images. But this leads us precisely to the position of the ACLU (whose membership and leadership have long benefitted from the historic Jewish advocacy of toleration) that there is and can be no crime in any mode of symbolic representation whatever, regardless of its content or its tenor, except in certain very narrowly construed contexts where words are conceded to amount to actions, *e.g.*, fraud, threat, extortion and debated cases of overt inducement of panic and incitement to riot. Certainly no verbal or non-verbal symbolic expression of a political belief or affiliation, no matter how hateful, should on this account ever be regarded as legally impermissible. The adoption of such a stance by the ACLU and other liberal bodies and individuals has of late forced a crisis of conscience on many Jews (and friends of Jews) who long have thought themselves pure liberals and yet have felt a revulsion in their bowels toward the extension of toleration to intolerance, and nonetheless found difficulty in discovering the moral principle upon which their revulsion logically or conceptually might be grounded.

Characteristically, because liberalism is a formal system with no inherent material values of its own, its account of the principles which ought to guide the formation of law abstracts from the material content of the values in question, and so naturally reaches the conclusion that the content of symbols is irrelevant to the propriety of their expression. The liberal position is predicated, in other words, upon the false assumption that symbols have no meaning.

It is true, to be sure, that symbols have meaning only with the aid of convention. Yet they do have meaning. And, in determining the moral acceptability of allowing symbols to be uttered, it might well be appropriate to examine their meaning. In the case of the swastika, for example, it is sometimes claimed that this ancient symbol has no intrinsic connection with Naziism, no intrinsic meaning whatsoever, unless perhaps some archetypal association with the idea of compactness. The suggestion is disingenuous. Meaning is never "intrinsic," always relational and thus associative. Once, by custom, convention, tradition, this and like symbols may have denoted compactness or some such generalized value notion. Today, in the nascent world-cultural consciousness, however vaguely, this symbol denotes just one thing, Naziism.

Not vaguely but precisely what does this mean? Its meaning has been defined (and was defined explicitly before the Nazi idea bore its deadly fruit in globally destructive action) by the theorists and ideologues of the Nazi movement and by the demonic architect of that movement himself. It refers to a system of ideas and emotions the purport of which, *inter alia,* is that it was right to murder six million Jews and would be still more right to murder the rest. It refers more broadly (as though wider generality were needed to make clear the universality of its viciousness) to the belief that violence is self-justifying.[26] It comes as close as possible within the realm of concrete expression, in other words, to the assertion of the radical transvaluation of values, the taking of good for evil and evil for good which Milton's Satan contemplated in his wrath but which Hitler transformed into the policy not only of a party but of an entire modern nation-state.

Liberalism, quaintly, does not condemn that transvaluation. Values, it claims are the object of any interest. Such a principle can afford no material basis for the condemnation of any particular values as such, although it may and does deplore the actual immolation or exploitation of the interest of some in behalf of what it takes to be that of others. From this point of view it will seem a matter of indifference what values in particular are paraded or (as in idolatry) celebrated. But from the perspective of a society which has chosen to pursue the highest good to the best of its ability and perception it will be a matter of the greatest moment which values are flaunted and which are flouted.

Judaism in its founding axiom does condemn the radical trans-valuation, and condemns it (because it recognizes the meaning of its symbolism) even as a mode of expression. This is what is meant by the condemnation of blasphemy.

The founding axiom of the Mosaic law is that expressing the reality of God, by which we understand the reality of Perfection. The most universal (and least understood) practical application of that fact, which expresses itself as an imperative upon all aspiring beings, is the obligation not to take the name of the Absolute God in vain. Popularly that is taken to mean that when we hit our thumbnail with a hammer instead of striking the tack at which we aimed we should say 'Oh my!' or even make some reference to excretion or coitus preferably to saying 'goddammit!' A misconstrusion, trivializing the commandment into a mere matter of words by failing or refusing to recognize that words have meaning.

But in the context of the Mosaic Torah 'God' has meaning. It means the absolute Perfection which calls forth in all aspiring beings a striving toward perfection and imposes on all conscious beings a moral obligation to pursue that obligation, *i.e.,* to seek perfection. To take the name of God in vain, to set it at nought—or, more precisely, to take it ill, to assign to it a value associated with evil—is to ignore the whole system of practical moral imperatives imposed by the Reality toward which that name orients us, to fail to be morally alive or to strive intellectually to ignore or morally to defy the imperatives so imposed. Taken in its full seriousness such setting at nought or "setting at ill" is outright to negate that system of imperatives, to deny the good and affirm the evil, or rather to advocate evil for its own sake and abhor good intrinsically. Such a posture is what is meant by blasphemy.

Of course, one may be literal and imagine that blasphemy consists merely in the utterance of impious words or symbols—rather as a child might make a rude or obscene gesture without quite knowing fully what it meant or even having the faintest notion of obscenity, or might draw a swastika without a glimmer of the enormity for which that symbol stands but only as a kind of witless defiance of a vaguely apprehended taboo. But that would not be blasphemy but only innocence or ignorance, or perhaps simply rudeness or bad taste. To blaspheme is to *use* the symbol (rather than simply mentioning it or quoting it, or say displaying it exploitatively for its shock value, as paperback publishers seem recurrently to do), to use it in a rather full awareness of the meaning it has been given by history *and to mean it in that sense,* that is to affirm evil in its most palpable, least ambiguous form, with full seriousness, desire and intent of execution, and to reject good absolutely. There is no reason why such an expression made with such intent should be countenanced in our public places.

It must often have puzzled students of the law why blasphemy was included among the Noahidic prohibitions, along with idolatry, sexual license, murder, rapine, the devouring of a member of a living beast and the lone positive injunction to institute some system of justice (*Sanhedrin* 56a). Why should mankind at large gentile as well as Jew be expected to pay lipservice to the Israelite God? This seems to derogate from the universality of the very concept of commandments applicable to all humanity. The answer, in terms of the preceding analysis is not difficult at all. What is called for is not verbal deference to the word 'God' without reference to its meaning (as some would spell it in English without its middle vowel—to show deference to the word) or the avoidance of making light of such a word. Rather what is demanded (as a general principle of the moral law) is the prohibition of the negation of all that the notion of God stands for and requires insofar as the notion of a Being of absolute perfection has regard to human affairs.

It might be supposed that no rejection of all principles of positive morality, love, kindness, gentleness, generosity, goodness, fairness, and honesty, for example, could be so sweeping as to give any sphere of concrete application to so broad a principle, that no one would wittingly negate all moral principles under the delusion that violence and cruelty, destructiveness, tyranny and terror could be taken as goods, indeed instituted as principles of rule and their opposites negated and rejected as inferior. But the fresh memory of the Nazi holocaust proves how wrong such a supposition would be.

Not surprisingly, in the realm of symbols to which historic usage and association have imparted objective meanings, there is an opposite to the swastika as a symbol of degradation, hatred, violence and destruction. That symbol is not, as might appear, the Magen David, for Naziism is not opposed to Judaism alone, but to all humane values, of which the prophets and sages of Israel have been eloquent and urgent but by no means wholly isolated spokesmen. The symbolism of the Magen David, the mystic hexagram of interlacing equilateral triangles oriented with bases and points towards heaven and towards earth, was explicated in the meditations upon it of Franz Rosensweig. It is emblematic of the interconnectedness and interaction of the transcendent with the here and now—of the relations between God and man, God and nature, man and man, man and nature. It is in this regard symbolic of the special task or mission of Israel to mediate the sanctity of the Transcendent into earthbound existence through ethics and spirituality, the love of God, love of man and love of nature.

But the rainbow is a more ancient and more universal symbol. Biblically interpreted as the sign of a universal covenant not with Israel alone but with rectifiable humanity, the "sons of Noah." This covenant does not demand a national mission borne through the generations by the surviving institutions of an integrated national culture. Rather the rainbow is taken Biblically as the visible manifestation of a pledged renunciation of global destruction by God (thus symbolic of the stabie order of nature) and of violence for its own sake by humanity. This bow (*keshet*) displaces the armorer's bow and marks an epoch in the human dissociation of violence from the divine. As the emotive paradigm of nature's stability and thus of harmony, growth, hope and the renunciation of violence as an end in itself, the rainbow is a fitting symbol of the universal (and minimal) divine covenant. For nature is the meeting ground of human and divine creative activity, where no particularistic forms of ritual or formal recognition of the Principal of nature are required, but God's acts can be emulated and in a way fulfilled through humanity's procreative expressions and nurturative/artistic endeavors toward the preservation and the cultivation of nature—including human nature. This becomes the human charge, first given to Adam and renewed to the sons of Noah and their progeny, to dwell in the world, to populate it, to tend it as a garden and perfect it (*letakken olam*), and along with it ourselves.

Of course, it may be said that such principles and signs as these, and their meanings and implications are beyond the ken of the law. But such an admission is prophetic of a tragic fate for any nation in which it must be made. For how can a system of laws survive which is constitutionally unable to recognize or deal with evil at its most palpable and least deceptive or disguised? Indeed, if our laws contain no principle which would allow the recognition and discouragement of the open celebration of evil for its own sake, but place all symbolisms on a par, then they are in a bad as well as an unstable state.

Our situation is very much like that of Jonah, when summoned to prophesy against Nineveh. His mission was not to make Jews of the inhabitants of the great city, but rather the more Noahidic task of summoning them back within the commonly recognized standards of moral decency, before their lawlessness and violence engulfed them in destruction. Like ours his task was largely educational—we must teach morals, we must not let the world forget what a Nazi is, what a swastika stands for, and, far more importantly, what values they oppose. Like many of us, Jonah was a latitudinarian, tolerant of the excesses of others so long as his own bunions were not trodden upon. He was quite content to let the Ninevans stew in their own juices, and had no desire to soil his public credibility with dire and far fetched sounding prophecies of doom—still less to appear in the gates of a great city as a moralist. But all this was predicated on neglect of what the Bible calls God's covenant with nature. For in Nineveh, as in our own world, there were many thousands of people who did not know their right hand from their left, but needed to be told—as well as a great deal of livestock.

To conclude, then. I have shown how moral rules are made possible in the monotheist conceptual framework. One final point remains and that is the elucidation of the fact that diverse environmental, social and cultural circumstances may call for modifications in the application of our rules. This does not mean that we can alter them to suit what we may regard as our convenience. Historically we adopt customs suited to our circumstances, not only functionally in the narrow, utilitarian sense, but symbolically, expressively: Customs too, like moral laws may be expressed as divine commands. But when they are, what is to be understood is only in part an aspiration toward divine Perfection. In part what is expressed by this idiom in this case is the apparent arbitrariness of the modality by which that aspiration is rendered concrete, defining the particularities of law and the usages of ritual and symbolism by reference to the circumstances of culture and the particularities of human needs and associations. These are retained and altered as we pass along, attached to new circumstances, modified or discarded, assigned new dimensions of meaning. They are never at a standstill while we live, and they are never radically at variance from one generation to the next as long as we retain language, history and the practice of rearing children. Customs fade, revive or die. But the great principles remain invariant. They are above the level of mores. They are norms and ideals. And expressive of the highest of these we have yet discovered/devised is the belief in the worth of human subjects as aspirants toward that perfection which is divine. It is this belief which is expressed normatively in the command 'Love thy fellow as thyself' and poetically in the words: 'God created man in His own image, in the image of God created him—male and female, created them.' (*Genesis* 1:27)

---

1. See FLEW'S *God and Philosophy* 1.15–18; *cf.* EMIL FACKENHEIM, *Encounters Between Judaism and Modern Philosopy, A Preface to Future Jewish Thought,* Philadelphia, 1973.
2. *God and Philosophy* 5.16.
3. *God and Philosophy* 9.15.
4. Mishnah *Sanhedrin* 10, allows a portion in the World to Come to the righteous of all

nations; *cf.* the dictum of the Sages which accords a two-fold reward to successful inquiry and a single reward to unsuccessful inquiry. Also see *Avot* 4:29, *Ta'anit* 7a, *Tosefta Sanhedrin* XIII 1,2; but contrast *Genesis Rabbah* 13:6.

5. See *A Treatise of Human Nature* Book III, Part I, Section I, ed. L. A. Selby-Bigge, Oxford, 1888 (1968), pp. 455–470; esp. p. 469: "I cannot forbear adding to these reasonings an observation, which may, perhaps, be found of some importance. In every system of morality, which I have hitherto met with, I have always remark'd, that the author proceeds for some time in the ordinary way of reasoning, and establishes the being of a God, or makes observations concerning human affairs; when of a sudden I am surpriz'd to find, that instead of the usual copulations of propositions, *is,* and *is not,* I meet with no proposition that is not connected with an *ought,* or an *ought not.* This change is imperceptible; but is, however, of the last consequence. For as this *ought* or *ought not,* expresses some new relation or affirmation, 'tis necessary that it shou'd be observ'd and explain'd; and at the same time that a reason should be given, for what seems altogether inconceivable, how this new relation can be a deduction from others, which are entirely different from it."

6. *Principia Ethica* IV 67, Cambridge, 1922 (1960), p. 114; *cf.* II.

7. *A Treatise of Human Nature,* ed. Selby-Bigge, p. 457, paragraph 2.

8. Similarly, Hume's remark that moralists may precede their moralizing by introducing "*a* God" is disingenuous. Had Hume encouraged his reader to dwell on diverse concepts of God and on the aptness or inaptness to morality of particular conceptions of divinity, rather than glossing over that point, the nexus between theology and ethics would not have appeared to be quite so arbitrary.

9. *On the Edge of the Primeval Forest,* London, 1948, 1956 (1922), 102; *cf.* p. 104.

10. GEORGE CATLIN, *Letters and Notes on the [Manners, Customs and Conditions of the] North American Indians,* ed. M. M. Mooney, New York, 1975 (London, 1841), pp. 236-7. Catlin's summary of his experience of the moral standards of the peoples among whom he travelled is a statement to which many another ethnographer here or elsewhere could subscribe: "I have roamed about visiting and associating with some three or four hundred thousand of these people, under an almost infinite variety of circumstances. From their very many and decidedly voluntary acts of hospitality and kindness, I feel bound to pronounce them, by nature, a kind and hospitable people. I have been welcomed in their country, and treated to the best that they could give me, without any charges made for my board. They have often escorted me through their enemies' country at some hazard to their own lives, and aided me in passing mountains and rivers with my awkward baggage. Under all of these circumstances of exposure, no Indian ever betrayed me, struck me a blow, or stole from me a shilling's worth of my property." p. 91.

11. See *An Examination of Sir William Hamilton's Philosophy,* 3rd ed., 1867, pp. 119–129, repr. as an appendix to Richard Taylor's ed. of MILL's *Theism,* Indianapolis, 1957, pp. 89–96.

12. This was the suggestive import of a lecture delivered by Gordon Kaufman under the auspices of the Charles Moore East-West Philosophers' Lecture Fund at the University of Hawaii, May 23, 1977.

13. See *Deuteronomy* 13:5, *Sotah* 14a; MAIMONIDES *Guide to the Perplexed* I 54, III 54 and Eight Chapters 5, 7.

14. See *Makkot* 23b; *cf.* MAIMONIDES *Sefer ha-Mitzvot,* The Positive Commandments, item 1, and The Negative Commandments, item 1.

15. See *Exodus* 12:49; *Cf. Leviticus* 24:22: "Ye shall have one justice (*mishpat*), stranger and homeborn alike, for I am the Lord your God." The passage clearly states that monotheism is the basis of the ethical concept of equity, as Hermann Cohen pointed out. The means by which the nexus is forged is in the provision, through God, of an objective standard against which subjective self-serving and preference for one's own can be tested and found wanting; *cf. Exodus* 23:1-12, *Leviticus* 19:34, *Deuteronomy* 1:16-17.

The Biblically instituted writing of the Law (*Exodus* 24:9, *Deuteronomy* 17:18, 31:9) and its public reading (*Deuteronomy* 31:10 ff.) regarded not only the familiarity of all with its principles but the conception of those principles as fixed and invariant in their application to all (*cf. Deuteronomy* 31:12).

16. *Leviticus* 19:33; *cf. Exodus* 22:20, 23:9, *Deuteronomy* 10:19. Once again, the reference to God is not otiose or rhetorical but a reminder of the perspective from which the stranger's worth is as great as one's own.

17. *Cf. Genesis* 4:23–24: "Lamech said to his wives:

> Adah and Zillah, hear my voice;
> Ye wives of Lamech, hear what I say.
> For I have slain a man for wounding me
> And a boy for bruising me.
> For if the vengeance in behalf of Cain be
>   sevenfold
> Then seven and seventyfold shall be my vengeance."

The Torah repeats the ancient boast not merely as a display of Lamech's hybris, but for the sake of the sharp contrast between his primitive assessment of worth in terms of power to inflict violence as compared with its own *moral* ethos: Thus the emphasis of *Leviticus* 24:17 ff.: "He that smiteth *any* man . . ."; *cf. Exodus* 21:25: The emphasis is on proportionality, not on retaliation; thus, where a slave is concerned, to whom monetary compensation proportional to the harm would be pointless, freedom is the price of injury. In all other cases, class or status is irrelevant and compensation for injury is based solely on the nature of the harm, not on the social standing of the victim. Similarly with regard to the special protection of the widow and the orphan (*Exodus* 22:24). Their humanity rather than their station imparts to them their deserts of kindness, and their helplessness makes them the subjects of special treatment—a complete reversal of the ethos and machismo of Lamech.

18. For further discussion of this issue, see my article on "Maimonides' Philosophy of Law," in the inaugural number of the *Jewish Law Annual,* 1978.

19. *Sociobiology,* Cambridge, 1975.

20. *Eruvin* 49a, *Ketubot* 103a, *Baba Batra,* 12b, 59a, 168a.

21. *Cf.* Lucretius *De Rerum Natura* II 1ff.

22. *Baba Metzia* 30b. *Cf.* the discussion in Elliot Dorff's article "The Interaction of Jewish Law with Morality," *Judaism* 26 (1977), pp. 456–459. Dorff cites Nachmanides as interpreting the Talmudic expression '*lifnim mi-shurat ha-din*' as referring to compromise. Concession might have been a better choice of word, less suggestive connotatively of the liberal presumption that the parties will even in this context inevitably be jockeying for position—which is exactly what the Sages say they must not do. Dorff lists '*kofin 'al middat Sedom*' as "the first" of the complementary moral concepts embedded in the Law, astutely, since it is an axiom on which the entire Law depends. But in our own analysis this axiom is not quite first (despite its arresting interest). Rather it is a corrolary of 'Love thy fellow as thyself,' which is in turn a concrete application at the interpersonal level of the general *mitzvah* of *homoiosis theoi,* becoming as like to God as humanly possible. The Rabbis regarded the claims of charity, for example, as actionable, although the precise demands of charity, etc. were not set by statute. Their resort to moral suasion or social pressure in cases where they judged the strict sentence of the law to be insufficient to the demands of equity may have been due more to lack of power than to fear of "importing too much of morality into the law." For the Law itself was not minimal in its demands. Thus "Rav held that conduct beyond the strict requirements of the law was actionable because it was, in fact, the law" as Dorff writes, in accordance with *Proverbs* 2:20 "That you may walk in the way of good men and keep the path of the righteous." Which is, as Maimonides and Nahmanides recognized, the social expression of the general mitzvah of *Leviticus* 19:2, "the locus classicus of imitatio Dei."

Of course the ability to "go beyond the strict sentence of the Law" requires an ability to see just what the intention of the Law is, lest one run against it rather than furthering it, and it requires an ability to see where concessions should be made and in what direction, without at the same time elevating the maxims of those concessions into new legal principles (which would only exacerbate the problem of potential conflict of laws and rights, which the principle of concessions ought to help to ameliorate)—but these two responsibilities, that of plumbing the intentions of the Law and that of probing the merits of situations, were juridical tasks which the Rabbis in their role as judges and legal judicial scholars (but never quite as legislators) were more than willing to undertake.

23. *Cf.* the article cited in note 18 above.

24. KANT, *Groundwork of the Metaphysic of Morals,* ch. 2, tr. H. J. Paton, New York, 1956, p. 80; *cf.* MAIMONIDES, *Eight Chapters,* 8, etc.; *cf.* SAADYA GAON, *Book of Beliefs and Opinions* IV, esp. iii and iv.

25. Descartes understood this when he argued that bodies can be known to exist external to the mind only with the aid of the assumption of the existence and absolute perfection (read as benevolence) of God. Correspondingly, there is no recognition of the objective reality of other minds without the same assumption, hence no possibility of their moral recognition. Of course I may resolve to behave *as though* I had reason to believe there were other persons in the world. But here, as was the case with the recognition of objects, causes, etc., it becomes questionable which is the fiction, the presumption that others exist or the notion that I am obviating any assumption of their reality by relying upon ideas which do not posit their existence and yet are parasitic upon the thought of their reality.

To escape the moral solipsism in which phenomenalism had trapped Heidegger, Buber gave primacy to encounter (a relational notion) above subject and object—relying upon (problematic and quasi-mystical) phenomenological grounds whose purchase on ontology was suppositious at best. Had he discovered grounds (in the coherence of experience, for example) for conceding the reality of the external world, at least as a likely story, phenomenalism might have become unnecessary, and the reality of God, as an essential part of the likely story, might have afforded a basis for moral recognition of others' subjecthood in realism rather than phenomenalism. Alternatively, a contingency argument which did not rest on the assumption of an external world might have been used to establish the existence of God, and that in turn serve in Cartesian wise as a ground for faith in external reality. In either case realism affords a more fitting outcome than does phenomenalism, since it says: 'I shall regard others as subjects, which they are' rather than saying: 'I shall regard others as though they were subjects,' or 'I shall regard others as though both they and I were ontically secondary to the encounter in which we meet'—For that last is a rather tenuous notion, whose specifiable moral content (if any) is slight, and that ambiguous, more suited in its ambiguity to the indirection of notes sent on pale stationery to dismissed lovers, or to sermons desirous of avoiding grappling with issues on all fours, than it is to the actual process of moral confrontation in which the subjecthood of others is admitted and accorded practical recognition—an ambiguity made plain by the ease with which the notion of confrontation was transformed in the 1960's from an ethical ideal into a euphemism for hostility and coercive intransigence of various kinds.

26. *Cf.* Uriel Tal in *Violence and Defense in the Jewish Experience,* edited by S. W. Baron, G. S. Wise and L. E. Goodman, J.P.S., 1977, pp. 205 ff.